Beyond the Numbers

AMERICAN ALLIANCE OF MUSEUMS

The American Alliance of Museums has been bringing museums together since 1906, helping to develop standards and best practices, gathering and sharing knowledge, and providing advocacy on issues of concern to the entire museum community. Representing more than 35,000 individual museum professionals and volunteers, institutions, and corporate partners serving the museum field, the Alliance stands for the broad scope of the museum community.

The American Alliance of Museums' mission is to champion museums and nurture excellence in partnership with its members and allies.

Books published by AAM further the Alliance's mission to make standards and best practices for the broad museum community widely available.

Beyond the Numbers

Budgeting for Museum Professionals

Kristine Zickuhr

ROWMAN & LITTLEFIELD
Lanham • Boulder • New York • London

Published by Rowman & Littlefield
An imprint of The Rowman & Littlefield Publishing Group, Inc.
4501 Forbes Boulevard, Suite 200, Lanham, Maryland 20706
www.rowman.com

86-90 Paul Street, London EC2A 4NE

British Library Cataloguing in Publication Information Available

Library of Congress Cataloging-in-Publication Data

Names: Zickuhr, Kristine, 1971- author.
Title: Beyond the numbers : budgeting for museum professionals / Kristine
  Zickuhr.
Description: Lanham, MD : Rowman & Littlefield Publishers, [2022] | Series:
  American alliance of museums | Includes index.
Identifiers: LCCN 2021055586 (print) | LCCN 2021055587 (ebook) | ISBN
  9781538156384 (cloth) | ISBN 9781538156391 (paperback) | ISBN
  9781538156407 (ebook)
Subjects: LCSH: Budget in business. | Museums—Economic aspects. |
  Museums—Employees. | Leadership.
Classification: LCC HG4028.B8 Z53 2022 (print) | LCC HG4028.B8 (ebook) |
  DDC 658.15/4—dc23/eng/20220113
LC record available at https://lccn.loc.gov/2021055586
LC ebook record available at https://lccn.loc.gov/2021055587

Contents

Preface

Once I was at a professional gathering and someone asked me what I do. I explained that I oversaw administration at a university art museum. When they asked what that meant, I said that I handled the things nobody else wanted to do, like budgeting. This was a phrase I used occasionally, but later that evening I stopped to think about it. I actually loved my job and thought areas like budgeting were powerful and interesting tools for museums. Why did I feel the need to minimize my work? How could I help others see the budgeting process as dynamic and engaging? What if I could invite others in, instead of feeling the need to downplay the role of budgeting? That's where the idea for the book began.

When I reviewed the existing literature, I was surprised to discover that there were virtually no books on museum budgeting. There are some high-quality books on museum administration but not a single one (that I could find) devoted to budgeting and its connection to strategy. In the museum field, we talk frequently about pay equity, accessibility, and a lack of funding, but we don't seem to talk about budgeting. Yet, the way that resources are managed is a direct cause of all of these issues, as well as a path to resolve them. I hope this book will be a small contribution to opening up that conversation.

Budgeting within a museum, or nonprofit institution, differs from budgeting within a for-profit business or corporation. While for-profit businesses may be genuinely interested in serving their customers, their ultimate goal is to make money. So, of course they pay careful attention to their income statements and balance sheets. It's part of their responsibility to their shareholders. Museums, on the other hand, emphasize public service and education. Our ultimate goal is to serve our audience. Some museum staff members bristle at the idea of integrating business practices and financial management from the corporate world. Yet, we have much to learn from how for-profit businesses manage their resources and measure their success. The metrics won't be the same, but leading with mission doesn't mean leaving the budget at the door. It's part of our responsibility to our stakeholders.

You might be surprised to discover that a book about budgeting doesn't contain many spreadsheets. You need spreadsheets, of course, but that's not where the magic actually happens. Instead, this book focuses on the larger issues related to budgeting. The chapters will help you identify your relationship to money, understand the dynamic ways budgets can serve museums, and see how budgeting connects to strategic planning. Then we'll actually get around to budgeting—discussing how to set up project and departmental budgets, as well as how they come together within a larger institutional budget. Then the fun really begins, and the next chapters focus on learning terminology, developing greater financial literacy, and discovering insights from your numbers. Finally, this book will address sustainability and how to make more out of your revenue, and how to get through a difficult financial situation.

This book is intended for everyone in the museum field but is designed to be accessible to people who have never looked at a budget in their lives. If you see little connection between a budget and your museum work or career, then this book is for you. If you hate or fear budgets, I hope I can help you see the value and satisfaction in creating and managing them. While all museum budgets have some commonalities, this book is particularly intended for museum professionals in small- and medium-sized government museums. This is where I've spent the majority of my museum career and I'm aware of the particular challenges (and opportunities?) present within the government budgeting process. These institutions are also less likely to have a large museum staff that includes individuals dedicated to financial management. Also, please be aware that while this book offers some concrete tools, it is not intended to offer advice regarding formal budget compliance or reporting standards. You can skip around the book if you'd like, but I recommend reading it in sequence, in order to progressively build up your knowledge. Don't be tempted to skip ahead to the section about cats on water skis.

And, if you do the quiet work of managing the operational side of a museum, I hope this book will offer some encouragement and inspiration. The work you do makes a difference to our field. And the next time you're at a professional function, when someone asks what you do, I hope you will answer that you manage one of the most dynamic and important parts of the museum: the budget.

I

CREATING SPARKS

1

✛

Finding Your Connection

As individuals and representatives of institutions, our relationship with money is complex. It can represent success and prosperity. It can be used responsibly to achieve our goals, create solid foundations for ourselves and our institutions, and help us serve our communities. In difficult times, it might be the only thing keeping the wolf from the door, providing security against institutional failure. For some, money has darker associations, and it may symbolize all that is bad with the world. We may equate money with greed and corruption. We may believe that funding has nothing to do with the important research and education that we do in museums. Money, and the strings that go with it, may even have the power to compromise our mission. These associations often relate to our personal relationship with money, how we grew up, whether we had financial security, and the type of values and experiences we have as adults.

If you think back to your earliest memories, you might find one relating to money. For me, I used to visit my godparents on their farm, and they would occasionally give me a silver dollar. At the time they weren't uncommon or particularly valuable, but I knew they were special. I was always secretly excited to see if they had one waiting for me. I loved their weight and shine. I knew they were different from "regular" money. I still have them and they're still not worth much more than a dollar. I would never sell them because their value was never about their monetary worth. But they take me back to my visits to their small farm and the excitement of receiving something that I could cherish and squirrel away. The fact that my godparents surprised me with them made me loved and valued. So, while it's a memory related to money, it's actually not about money at all.

On a professional level, we may have a negative association with budgeting because we work in a field with limited resources. Budgets may feel restrictive or punitive. The process may feel dry and lifeless. We may have worked at institutions that suffered budget cuts, staff reductions, or even closures. Or we may just be so removed from financial management at our institutions that it seems alien or irrelevant. On a professional level, you may have encountered difficulty in negotiating for salary, or may not feel adequately compensated for the work you do. You might feel frustrated that the work you love isn't necessarily financially rewarding. If this is the case, it may take time to undo those associations and create a more positive relationship with money. If you can think back, you may also associate money with joyful moments in your life or career. That big grant you landed for your museum or the generous gift from a donor that funded a public program. Maybe you even successfully negotiated a pay increase or helped advocate for pay equity in your institution.

As you can see, associations with money are very personal. We're the ones who imbue it with meaning. Whatever reaction it evokes, we can't deny that money has a profound impact on our lives and our institutions. By acknowledging the tremendous influence money plays in our lives, our societies, and our world, we can begin to own our responsibility to advocate for our organizations. By tapping into the knowledge of how money works, we can harness its positive qualities for the good and make adjustments when it doesn't fully reflect our values. We can never forget that managing money isn't actually about money.

One of the biggest barriers to empowerment is knowledge. You might be an expert in your own area, but struggle with financial terminology or the budgeting process. If you're new to budgeting, it may seem intimidating or confusing. You might wonder if you're "doing it right." I hope I can reassure you that anyone can learn to read and create a budget! Budgeting is a learned skill, just like most others. No one was born a curator, and no one was born a financial specialist. While it's true that a background in administration or financial management may make budgeting easier, people from all backgrounds can learn how to read, set up, and manage a simple budget.

We sometimes have a misconception that some people are analytical while others are creative, but that they can't be both. This couldn't be further from the truth. In reality, there's a bit of creativity involved with budgeting and bit of structure involved with creative pursuits. You can even "budget creatively" (and this doesn't mean cooking the books!). We can expand our potential when we stop putting ourselves into small buckets. We might say, "I'm not a numbers person" or "I'm a right brain person." This is a way of selling ourselves short. Maybe you struggled with a budget in the past or sat in a budget meeting with your eyes glazing over because you couldn't follow the conversation. If you're honest with yourself, you might even discover that resistance to budgeting is a way of elevating yourself above the "bean counters" of the world (bean counters unite!). Perhaps you secretly feel this is just someone else's job and you can't be bothered. Or that you're much too creative to understand all of those numbers on the page. Or maybe you really do want to learn and just don't know where to begin.

In all of our interactions with money, we have a choice about whether we will engage. Even if a budget is imposed on you from above, you may have the choice to revamp it or influence the process so that it better meets your objectives. If your own personal or professional financial situation isn't ideal, you can work on increasing your skill and comfort level with budgeting. Money is a tool to serve us, not vice versa. Owning and embracing that responsibility can be part of a choice you're making as a professional, on behalf of yourself and your institution.

Why Does Budgeting Matter?

The word "budget" tends to evoke visions of spreadsheets and columns of numbers. But budgets aren't just numbers on a page. They're people, programs, exhibitions, and collections. They're the hopes of the institution and its community. They're the funding for a family program and the solace of a quiet gallery in a chaotic world. Numbers can also represent loss, when a favorite public program is cut, valued staff members are laid off, or a museum closes. There can be grief and joy behind numbers. Once you make the connection between a budget and the people and programs behind it, you might never view it as a stale document again. If the upcoming budget meeting was actually a meeting about the people you serve and the programs you provide, would you infuse that discussion with more energy and interest? Budgeting is advocacy in action.

Other than its staff, funding is one of the most powerful resources a museum has available. By managing it effectively, you can leverage funds to their greatest potential, using every dollar strategically. It's relatively easy for an institution to create a lofty strategic plan that talks of accessibility and community service. Most of us have one. The plan may include tangible goals and initiatives that move the institution in the right direction. The budget, however, tends to lag behind strategic planning. Yet, more so than any other document, it reveals the institution's true priorities and investments. A budget might even unknowingly reveal a museum's priorities. Do you want to know what a museum really values? Look at the budget.

This also makes it a powerful tool for change. If you create your budget as an *outcome* and driver of your planning, it will begin to naturally reflect and support your priorities. If, on the other hand, the budget carries over year to year with little thought, it can reflect outdated institutional priorities and structures. This is not unusual, and many museums do rubber-stamp their budget each year. Some may not even have a budget at all. Yet, the budget can be a vehicle for achieving our institutional vision.

Budgets Are Moral Documents

How we use resources, where they're allocated, and the values they reflect mean that budgets are moral documents. There's an inherent morality in deciding how to distribute resources. In the museum field, we often talk about a lack of funding, salary inequities, and the urgent call to become more accessible to our communities. Yet, we rarely talk about how budget and resource management connect to those issues. We rarely talk about budgets at all. Yet, equity and accessibility concerns don't occur in a vacuum. People (or, more often, groups of people over time) are making decisions that result in these outcomes. Someone has decided how to structure salary ranges. Someone else decided that funding should support a particular exhibition over another. Someone still believes that internships don't have to be paid, because the museum is short on funding and there's a waiting list of interested graduates. Someone has determined that the museum lobby should be cavernous, sterile, and intimidating. Or that changing that legacy isn't a priority. Sadly, someone might even still think they can hire a female director and pay that person less than a comparably qualified male candidate. Nearly all of the issues we talk about in the museum field are a direct result of how funds and other resources are, or aren't, employed. How they're managed and who has the power to manage them. If these issues matter to you, then budgeting should also matter to you.

Another reason to care about budgeting is that taking good care of resources tends to attract more resources. This isn't a new-age concept but rather a practical observation. As institutions and individuals, we excel at the things we focus on and nurture. If we tend to our budgets and show them the care they deserve, they'll support us in return. This approach is more apt to draw positive attention and bring us more of these resources to manage. Consider your perspective if you were a granting organization or a prospective donor. Would you be more likely to provide funding to an organization with a well-prepared budget that mirrored their priorities and a track record of effective use of funding? Wouldn't you be impressed if you could actually see the institution's values demonstrated in their budget? That type of application would be much more successful than a hard-luck story from an underfunded museum. While it may sound harsh, funders and donors want to support an institution that is already successful and well-regarded. They may give a hand up to organizations that show future promise, but they definitely don't want to be embroiled in a financial scandal or associated with a failing institution. They have to trust that the organization knows how to maximize and shepherd its funding. This is particularly critical for public museums, who hold collections and institutions in the public trust. If you take care of the dollars under your care, demonstrating good stewardship and effective leverage of your resources, you'll draw the attention and respect of parent agencies, funders, granting agencies, and legislators. When tough decisions are made about budget priorities, these stakeholders may shield your institution from cuts and even send other dollars your way. This isn't a "bootstrap" philosophy, by the way. We can't just wish ourselves into prosperity or work a little harder and make it so. Many museums will face shortfalls and funding difficulties despite their best efforts. And, much like people, some institutions have privilege born of large endowments or well-connected donors. But establishing a culture of financial literacy and good stewardship will benefit *every* institution, regardless of their individual situation.

Proficiency with budgeting can help a museum thrive during good times, but it can also help it survive during more difficult phases. A solid budgeting process can help you see where to make reductions, if ever necessary, and help ensure that your remaining funding is working overtime to serve your mission. Museums that manage effectively during difficult times have a good understanding of their resources and the programs they support. If you're fortunate to work within an institution that has adequate funding, you may become complacent about the need to manage resources effectively. If you're not already crystal clear on your budget priorities during good times, you may go off course when you do need to tighten up. If your budget is a mess or you're drifting financially, take the opportunity to address it before it becomes urgent.

On an individual note, developing a basic understanding of how budgets work can make museum professionals more effective in their careers. It can make you a stronger advocate and make your skills more valuable to your institution. As you progress within the museum field, it's increasingly likely that you'll be asked to create and manage a budget. This expectation often comes with little guidance or oversight regarding how a budget is created. Demonstrating an interest in, and proficiency with, financial management will also offer you greater participation in the strategic direction of your institution. You can put your head in the sand if you want, but you might pop back out to find that your section or department has been passed over. The best way to advocate is to have an understanding of how resources are distributed and managed. This doesn't mean making unrealistic demands or advocating at the expense of other sections. Although, if you do want to do that, you'll also benefit from financial literacy! But ideally it means identifying the best time and approach to secure resources for your program or institution. It will help you become a proactive partner in securing resources and making decisions about how they're allocated. It will also aid you in making *strategically* timed requests for raises or greater responsibility in your position. Knowing *when* to ask is just as important as how, and it will make you more successful, I promise! As we all know, the museum field has become more competitive. Being a budget wizard (or at least an apprentice) is an advantage during the recruitment process, *no matter what type* of position you're interested in. If you're in, or hope to be in, a senior position within a museum, this knowledge will make you a more effective leader. Not only because financial management itself is important but also because understanding the *strategy* behind management of resources is key. Your job might be to manage collections, educational programs, exhibitions, or facilities, but we all benefit from knowing how to manage a budget.

Finally, I might even try to persuade you that learning a new skill is a satisfying and interesting experience in itself. I won't deny that it's harder as we get older, but it becomes even more important to keep our minds moving and expanding in new directions. Sometimes it's tempting to fall back on the expertise we've acquired in our own realm of knowledge. It's hard to admit vulnerability, to not know the answers, or to make mistakes. This is particularly true in leadership positions where we might feel we need to pretend we know everything. Instead of asking about what we don't understand, we may gloss over the subject or even act like it isn't relevant to our work. Or maybe we're just so engrossed in our own area that there doesn't seem to be time to learn something new. We can benefit from stretching and challenging ourselves, however. And if you have no experience with budgeting at all, consider yourself fortunate. You have a whole new world to explore!

Whatever your background and perspective, I hope that some of these reasons will resonate with you and create a spark. Budgets can offer so much more than numbers on a page. Whether we like it or not, finances underpin the success of our institutions and initiatives. They directly connect to the strategic direction of our institutions and the values we try to uphold. They even impact the most important issues in the museum field such as accessibility, equity, and social justice. By engaging more dynamically with budgeting, you can become a stronger advocate for yourself and others. It will benefit your current institution and even your own career. You might even find it fun and exciting (please, look me up!).

Three Ways to Expand Your Financial Knowledge:

1. Try to identify your personal associations and memories associated with money. Can you recall times when money served you or your community, or brought you joy?
2. When you think about budgeting, what are the three words that first come to mind? Do they provide any insight into how you manage money in your personal or professional life?
3. Identify one or two motivations for increasing your knowledge of budgeting.

2

✢

Budgeting Is Dynamic

The word "dynamic" is defined as a process characterized by constant change or progress. It can also be a noun, a force stimulating change or progress. It might surprise you to think of budgeting as dynamic. Yet, at their best, budgets are living documents that can change over time, adapt to different workplace cultures, serve the needs of different stakeholders, and support shifts in strategic plans. The budgeting process itself can also be dynamic and full of energy and new ideas. But budgeting is also *a* dynamic, a force that can stimulate progress within a museum. A budget is an outcome of planning, but it's also a powerful tool, in itself, for advancing the evolution of an organization. I might even make the argument that budgets are more important than strategic plans, because they're the generators of tangible and measurable change. They're also highly adaptable, and the process can be adjusted to support a variety of workplace cultures, individual perspectives, and financial scenarios.

The Process Is the Product

The idea that budgets are dynamic flies in the face of a common misconception, that they're static, or even dry, documents. That they're punitive or restrictive. Maybe this is why so many people dislike or avoid budgeting. If you start to think of budgeting as a *process*, rather than a document, it opens up a new perspective. A budget is a document, but budget*ing* is the process behind it. One of my mentors, Sherry Kafka Henry, often says, "the process is the product." Sherry is a brilliant, creative museum consultant who helped our organization create an ambitious interpretive plan for a new museum. She would schedule work sessions where staff members and visitors could just drop in and out, and we would spend all day talking about relevant books and exhibitions. Guest curators and scholars stopped in to have lunch or participate in brainstorming. For some of us, it was difficult initially because we didn't have meeting agendas or clear objectives. It wasn't how our meetings were normally run. We were impatient and didn't know where the process was heading. Weren't we supposed to be creating an interpretive plan instead of sitting around talking about a book or article someone had read? Yet, some amazing (and actionable) concepts came out of those sessions because of the creative, workshop-style atmosphere. We came to understand that if we wanted innovative ideas, they weren't going to come out of a tightly scheduled one-hour meeting. We had to give the process time to unfold and include people who weren't normally around the table. At that time, I thought "the process is the product" was an interesting phrase, but I hadn't really internalized it. Then one day it was like a light went on. Yes, of course, the process *is* the product.

One way to interpret this is that the quality and character of the process will determine the quality of the end product. This is absolutely true. If you rush or minimize a planning process, you're unlikely to come out with a high-quality result. But it goes even deeper. It means that the most important aspect of your product actually *is* the process of creating it. It's the planning, thinking, and discussion that goes into the budget. It's honoring budget*ing*, as a verb, not a noun. It gives shape to your final form, but the process has tremendous value in itself. The fact that it may be messy or contentious is exactly the point. The discussions and decisions themselves will help you better understand and define your institutional priorities. You'll come to appreciate the perspectives of others, what they value, what they worry about, and what they want to achieve. So, to allow it to be as dynamic as it can be, give the budgeting process the time and energy it deserves. I'm not suggesting that budgets be done in a full-day work session, where people drop in and out, sit on the floor, or kick off their shoes—although that might be fun for some of us. But if budgeting is confined to a short meeting that everyone rushes through, you might be missing out on some of the more interesting and valuable aspects of budgeting.

Budgets Are Forward-Looking

To understand why budgets are so dynamic and tied to the future success of an institution, it may be helpful to clarify what a budget is and how it's used. Sometimes, there's confusion about the difference between financial accounting and budgeting. While the terms are occasionally used interchangeably by people who work outside the field, there's an important distinction between them. Financial accounting is backward looking. It almost always consists of reporting and categorizing transactions that have *already* occurred. Other than informing you about trends and obligations, it can't help you plan the future. If you look up a past expense or review financial statements, you're relying on financial accounting. Financial accounting and reporting are valuable tools for checking in on budgets, but they're not budgeting. Budgeting, on the other hand, is *forward*-looking, creating a plan for how funding will be used in the future. It's all about where the institution is heading not where it has been. This, by its nature, means that a budget will change and evolve over time (unless we can predict the future perfectly). This is not a flaw and is, in fact, how the best budgets are designed to function. This dynamic, forward-looking perspective also reflects budgeting's strong connection to institutional planning and priorities. Healthy institutions evolve and grow in response to changes in the world around them. A museum that doesn't adapt will eventually fade away. So, institutional budgets should also evolve and adapt. They should be as flexible and dynamic as the institution they support.

Budgets Can Mirror and Support Change

Due to their dynamic nature, budgets easily adapt to changing circumstances. They can, and usually should, change over time. Budgets are just projections, of course; they're not plans set in stone. Change can occur over the short term, such as a quarter or a fiscal year, and this is especially the case when taking a longer view. A budget can tell you a lot about how the museum has evolved. If your budget hasn't changed significantly in a long time, it's a sign that something else in your institution might be stuck. It means you're doing things the way you always have. This can point to a larger issue of strategic planning being stagnant or nonexistent. More likely, it means that your budget is not keeping pace with your planning. Or maybe you're not challenging your institution to grow its capacity. This can be true on the expense side, such as creating new programming opportunities, marketing material, or conservation initiatives. It can also be true for revenue, such as creating a new source of funding or seeking major grants. Whatever the case, a stagnant budget suggests that change hasn't been a priority at your institution.

A budget, and an institutional plan, can change for many reasons—a leader transitions, a programming opportunity arises, or the museum responds to a developing social or health issue. Some of these situations may be internally initiated, but others are externally imposed. And some can be predicted, while others catch us by surprise. Depending on the severity and scale, they have a dramatic effect on an institutional budget with relatively little warning. This means that a budget created in July might look very different by April. The entire museum field experienced this in 2020, when the COVID-19 pandemic rapidly and dramatically affected budgets in most institutions. All of the careful planning invested in budgeting was almost meaningless. During a call with fellow museum administrators, we joked that perhaps the best approach to budgeting would involve a dart board. This is an extreme example, but it demonstrates how difficult it can be to predict the future. More often, plans and budgets change for smaller reasons—more events have been booked, vendor prices have increased, or staff members have transitioned, for a few examples. These are more subtle shifts, but, if they're significant enough, they may be valid reasons to adjust a budget as well. In any case, you can be fairly sure that the budget you create won't perfectly capture the expenses you eventually incur. Your goal will be to keep it in on the dart board, not to nail the bullseye.

Budgets Can Adapt to Different Institutional Cultures

Budgets are also dynamic in serving a variety of functions for a variety of people. If budgets don't seem meaningful to you, you may just need to find the right lens. A financial manager might be most interested in fiscal sustainability, primarily making sure that budgets are balancing expenses against resources. A director has a much different perspective and may be checking in on the institution's direction and key initiatives. She may want the high-level view and has a responsibility to be sure the institution is remaining financially sustainable. A board member might be interested to see the budget projections for her favorite initiative that she helped fund last year. She may use the information to decide if she'll provide additional funding for the coming year. A retail manager is focused on the projections for earned revenue and if he can improve the bottom line. And a governing agency might need to see revenue projections for the next three years so they can filter up to the larger organization for their own planning. This is part of the magic of budgeting (yes, I said "magic" and "budgeting" in the same sentence). Even the same budget can be adapted to a wide range of uses and needs. If you're new to budgeting, it can be helpful to consider your own perspective when you read, or eventually create, a budget: What matters to you and can you gain insight about it through the budget process at your institution?

Not only can budgets serve a variety of needs within, and beyond, an organization, they also can suit a wide variety of types of museums and work cultures. A misconception I've encountered is that budgeting somehow hampers creativity or is in opposition to the "real work" of the museum. A museum director once told me that he was reluctant to implement budgeting across the institution because he wanted it to remain agile. As a result, even senior staff members had no idea where their initiatives fit within the overall budget. Some project budgets were outlandish and others weren't ambitious enough. Although the museum was doing well financially, he didn't want staff members to be involved in the budgeting process. He was afraid that asking people to live within a budget would make them less creative, because they would become too conscious of funding considerations. I took his concerns seriously but helped persuade him that, if used effectively, a budget can actually uphold and promote creativity, not restrict it. And being flush with funding isn't a guarantee of creativity, either. Sometimes awareness of financial concerns (if they exist) can even become a creative challenge, leading people to find even better, lower-cost solutions. And if there aren't financial concerns, then reassuring staff members of strong financial support can be liberating. The push and pull between funding and creativity isn't always straightforward.

Even so, it's important to acknowledge the culture of an institution (and its leadership) when creating a budget process. After giving it some thought, I realized that this director's priorities were creativity and agility. If we didn't incorporate those concerns, he would be less likely to sponsor and support the budgeting process. So, we created a style around those values. For example, a pot of money could be left unassigned until the right opportunity came along. Staff members might be invited to create proposals for how to use the funding, which could lead to interesting discussions and debate. Or each section or department might be provided with a small surplus that they could use as they see fit to expand and develop new ideas within their area. Section managers could reallocate their own budget throughout the year, as long as it didn't exceed the overall approved amount. This would also create increased awareness of the budget without creating a sense of restriction. Here, the budgeting style could not only allow creativity, it could also facilitate it!

In another situation, a director was concerned about financial sustainability. A series of government funding decreases had taken a toll on the museum's revenue. This director was concerned that without tighter control, the museum could slip into deficit. It was building new sources of revenue, but the planning would take some time. Here, financial sustainability was the most important value for an organization. The organization needed to survive and stabilize before it focused on creativity and agility. In this case, the budgeting style had to be much more stringent and disciplined. There was no magic pot of money and the museum couldn't afford overages. And while the director didn't want to alarm staff members, she felt that transparency was important. Staff members were challenged to find ways to cut their section spending by a small percentage, while still serving the public in creative ways. Budget reviews were implemented on a more frequent basis, so that the senior staff could check in and stay on course. More budget information was shared so they had a better understanding of the situation, and also didn't worry excessively or make up stories in their head about what was occurring. While there wasn't a lot of extra funding, budget managers found that the allocated amounts were sufficient when carefully managed. Here, the budgeting style served as a short-term check and allowed the museum to get back on track. This was a difficult situation, but the budget process served as a vehicle for greater transparency and cohesion across the institution.

As the above examples show, there are many ways to approach a budgeting process. The point is that your style of budgeting should support your institutional priorities and culture. It might shift over time as the institution and leadership changes. Adjusting and adapting the process, rather than resenting or ignoring it, will go a long way toward creating a budget that you can understand and implement successfully. Sometimes resistance to budgeting is based in a mismatch to the institutional culture. You might even find ways to use budgeting to improve communication, promote transparency, and generate creativity. It's worth taking the time to assess and improve your institution's budgeting style if it isn't currently mirroring your values. You may find that it can actually advance, rather just coexist with, your culture and mission.

Adapting a budget process to an institutional culture also applies to how a budget is created and managed. Who's making the decisions and how are those communicated? Often this will mirror the hierarchical structure of the organization. In some institutions, the budget will only involve staff members at the senior leadership level or within the parent organization. The budget may be released in final form, and staff members will simply be expected to live within its parameters. For boards with fiscal responsibility, those members might have input or even complete authority over development or approval of the budget. Staff members may only see a small piece of the pie. In other institutions, it's a much more collaborative process, where multiple staff members provide input. It might involve months of discussion and even debate. Section, or even subsection, budgets might filter up for inclusion in the overall budget. Both approaches have their benefits and drawbacks. In a top-down approach, the decisions are clear and the budget is likely to mirror the strategic plan. There's no question about who has authority over budget decisions. This approach might even be required by governing documents or procedures. On the other hand, the decision makers might not have direct knowledge of the needs and priorities of sections of the institution. They may overlook opportunities or risks when creating budget projections. And it might not create enough accountability and engagement for the staff members who actually manage the budget. They may become complacent about the need to manage resources effectively. In a collaborative approach, there is more buy-in, more perspectives are represented, and the people who live within the budget have a larger voice in creating it. They have more involvement, so they might develop a shared sense of responsibility for understanding and managing the budget. On the negative side, too many opinions and priorities can lead to a lack of clarity. It can be disorganized and take a long time to plan a budget. If there's no clear method of establishing funding priorities, the process can become competitive and divisive. Resources might be allocated to the section with the loudest voice, rather than the section with the greatest need. There's no right or wrong way to create a budgeting process, as long as it serves your institution.

Budgets Can Create Consensus, or Confusion

The dynamic nature of budgeting is a positive thing, but it also means that there's a lot of variability and a lack of consistent process across the museum field. This may be one of the reasons why so little is written and shared about the museum budgeting process. While there are things that many museum budgets have in common, there is also significant variability across institutions. Sometimes these are based on internal decisions, but they may also originate in the policies or requirements of the parent organization. In the museum field, we may also structure a budget document to comply with the reporting requirements of professional organizations. This variance is why it's so important to establish good communication and documentation around the creation and maintenance of budgets and financial reports. It requires caution when comparing our own budgets or financial metrics to those of another institution. Someone wise once said that the key to reading a financial report is the notes at the bottom of the page. If you read the numbers without the context, you'll miss a lot and you might even reach erroneous or incomplete conclusions. This is because budgets are based so heavily on assumptions and interpretations. Here's an example of how two very similar institutions can reach very different budget numbers:

> *Expenses Consolidated*: Museum A hosts approximately three small traveling exhibitions each year, with lease fees totaling $50,000. Much of the other activity in the museum rotates around their schedule and themes. The education section plans a series of events around the exhibitions, which include live entertainment, food and drink, and hands-on activities. These are budgeted at $40,000. Opening events also require extra security, a service arranged by the administrative section of the museum for $10,000. These activities and services are all closely related to exhibitions, so the costs are considered part of the exhibition budget. As a result, Museum A budgets $100,000 annually for exhibitions. This puts their spending in the highest 25 percent of their peer institutions.

Expenses Distributed: Museum B also hosts three traveling exhibitions each year. These exhibitions have comparable lease fees, totaling $50,000. Just like Museum A, the education section plans opening night activities, and the administration section arranges for extra security. In Museum B's budget, however, these expenses are assigned to those respective sections. As a result, Museum B budgets only $50,000 for exhibitions. This puts their exhibition spending in the lowest 25 percent of their peer institutions. Yet, they also budget $40,000 for education and $10,000 for extra security, totaling $100,000.

These two examples show how dramatically interpretation and context can alter our view of a budget number. The two budgets look very different, yet they represent nearly identical activities and expenses. Of the two examples, neither approach is correct or incorrect, or even common or uncommon across the museum field. It really doesn't matter that much, as long as the museum itself is clear about what it's projecting and measuring. This is why the notes are key. If you have section budget managers in your museum, they need clarity about what expenses they're managing.

This issue also frequently comes up during benchmarking activities. Large professional organizations will gather data from hundreds of museums, so you can be sure that some of those numbers represent different things. If you're creating a survey, it will help create clarity (and better data) if you define how the numbers are defined and should be compiled. If you're reporting numbers, ask questions to gain clarity about what should be included (for the sake of your own institution and the entire field). If you do compare your institution to another, use these surveys with caution, and be sure you're using comparable measures or know to adjust them. Until the field speaks a "common language" in budgeting, surveys can create significant confusion and misleading information about the financial structure of the museums represented.

Budgets Are Dynamic *(but you still have to write them down)*

As we've seen, budgets are dynamic and can adapt to a wide variety of institutions, workplace cultures, and stakeholders' needs. They change over time in order to support new strategic plans or manage unexpected situations. The fact that budgets are dynamic, however, is not an excuse to not create one. You'll need a starting point, a commitment, a roadmap. Then you can adjust the budget as you go along. I like to think of the budgeting process as a road trip. There might be a certain appeal to setting out without a plan. Such freedom and spontaneity! We're not going to be "encumbered" by maps. But if you've ever actually done this, you might have found that you were soon lost, hungry, and tired—with no hotels available because it was Labor Day weekend. (Yes, this happened to me.) You might get lucky and take a great road trip without a plan; but, unless you have unlimited time and funding for gas, you'll probably want to choose a destination before getting in the car.

Most of us now have map applications on our phones that can guide us and even readjust the route when we get off track. Think of the budget process in a similar way. The map doesn't prevent you from stopping or changing your route.

In fact, it will get you back on track to your destination. During your journey, you might see something of interest that is a little out of the way. Or maybe something unexpected happens like a flat tire and you get behind schedule. You might even decide you want to change where you're going. And that can be accommodated, too. Just like using a map on a trip, a budget is a tool to help you get where you're going. Don't be so overwhelmed or reluctant to put things down on paper that you have no map at all.

And while it's important to give the planning process time to unfold, eventually putting things in writing has a way of solidifying and clarifying your intentions. Creating a written plan and institutional budget creates consensus around the direction of the organization. As we've seen, the process and format of budgets can vary significantly by institution. If budgets aren't in writing, staff members may have different expectations and interpretations of the decisions that were made. There's also value to committing plans on a written page. Somehow, it helps us manifest them. As an example, I was required to create a professional five-year plan for a course I was taking. I initially found it difficult to put my goals in writing. One of the goals I eventually identified was to write professionally. It honestly seemed far-fetched at the time. Yet, not long after I had put these plans in writing, I saw a call for book proposals and responded. If I hadn't put this goal on paper, I really don't think I would have noticed the opportunity. For me, this confirmed that writing down goals and plans somehow captures intentions and solidifies them. You still have to do the work, of course, but it creates a clear direction. This is particularly important when managing a budget. You can change it eventually, if needed, but don't underestimate the power of putting it on paper. The format of a written budget can, of course, be adapted to a variety of needs and preferences.

Three Ways to Expand Your Financial Knowledge:

1. Describe your museum's budgeting process in three words. For example, transparent or opaque, interesting or boring, accessible or confusing.
2. Describe your museum's culture or important values in three words.
3. Are the two sets of words similar? If not, identify some small, concrete steps you can take to bring your core values into the budgeting process.

3

✢

Relating Budgeting to Strategic Planning

Now you might be convinced that budgeting is dynamic, but how does the process relate to other institutional planning? Two of the most important planning processes for a museum are budgeting and strategic planning. These two processes and plans ideally work together, but they have unique purposes and perspectives. If strategic plans are the "why," then budgets are a big part of the "how." Both are necessary to create a successful institution. When these processes are aligned, they can create a powerful base for stability and evolution. When they're not, they can undermine each other and create a lack of cohesion across the institution. Strategic plans are big and broad! They start with large ideas. When we're fortunate and persistent, those ideas filter down to smaller building blocks of concrete goals and initiatives. Budgets are the opposite; they're built out of small and focused plans, which filter up to a larger plan for managing resources. At some point, these two processes have to intersect, with the strategic plan becoming gritty enough to actually enact and the budget becoming aspirational and flexible enough to support it. Getting them to work together is challenging but creates a balanced and powerful approach to planning.

Different Natures

Aligning budgeting and strategic planning requires an acknowledgment that they have very different purposes and perspectives. Museums have invested a great deal of time and energy into strategic planning over the past few decades. Strategic planning is an important process for furthering the museum's mission and vision. Yet, a strategic plan has limitations. A strategic plan is aspirational in nature. It inspires the staff and stakeholders and codifies the institution's highest values. We might think of a strategic plan as an eagle on an inspirational poster; it soars effortlessly through the sky. It's relatively easy to create a strategic plan because it's just that, only a plan. The details look blurry when you're ten thousand feet in the air. It's kind of fun to dream big. It's much harder to see a strategic plan to fruition. I'm sure most of us have gone through a strategic planning process, feeling energized and excited, only to look back a few years later with no idea what happened to the plan. It doesn't guide day-to-day decisions and we may not even remember what was on it. It's really easy to get caught up in all of the important ideas that come out of a strategic planning session. Accessibility! Audience Growth! Yes, but now what? It turns out that supporting a strategic plan with staffing and funding is actually kind of hard.

If a strategic plan is an eagle, then a budget might be more like a turtle. At first glance, it's not particularly inspirational. But if you look closer, you'll see the beautiful details, the adaptations that allow a turtle to survive, the strong shell that protects the institution. And while an eagle soars through the sky up above, a turtle moves slowly across the ground. It's hard for the turtle to keep pace with an eagle. Sometimes it's even hard for a turtle to figure out where it is within the greater landscape. The turtle is slow and steady and carries on his way. A turtle also carries the legacy of an institution, which is valuable, but can contain the remnants of former priorities, unexamined and carried ahead year after year. These are those programs that aren't working anymore, but no one can bear to cut.

There's a fable involving an eagle and a turtle that might be relevant when thinking about the nature of strategic planning and budgeting. The turtle is frustrated by how slowly it moves along the ground and would rather soar high above the earth. Ignoring its own nature, it convinces the eagle to pick it up and carry it into the air. While the turtle is initially awed by the view, he eventually struggles and falls. In darker versions, the eagle drops him. In others, the turtle opens his mouth to say something and falls (probably talking about the importance of budgeting). Whatever happened to the poor turtle, this is a good analogy for our comparison to strategic plans and budgets. Strategic plans are made to soar. Turtles are made to crawl. Both are valuable and beautiful creatures. Instead of trying to change their nature, we should respect what both have to offer our institutions. They must work together, however, which is a challenge given their different nature.

Once you think of strategic plans and budgets in this way, it's easy to understand why they get out of step with each other. They're vastly different in perspective. The nature and purpose of the planning process is different. The timeline and pace aren't usually in step. A strategic plan tends to take a longer view, typically three to five years. A truly strategic budget might also look several years out, but usually the focus is on a one-year horizon. In challenging times, we might only be projecting a quarter ahead. So, strategic planning can and should forge ahead and inspire us with those big picture initiatives, but the planning may need to circle back and make sure budgeting is coming along.

This is also complicated by the fact that the two plans have different purposes and sponsors. Directors tend to champion strategic plans because they're an embodiment of a vision for the organization. Individuals in these positions also tend to be transformational leaders who bring others along with them. They often want the institution to evolve to be even bigger and better. Great directors also understand and value budgeting, but most of their time is rightfully focused on high-level initiatives. A strategic plan inspires, but it typically doesn't direct the nitty-gritty operation of the organization. Budgets, on the other hand, are more commonly overseen by financial officers, deputy directors, or administrative managers. Leaders at this level may have a vision as well but, by necessity, they're more focused on practical applications. It's harder to inspire excitement about a budget. Both strategy and tactic are important to the success of an organization: vision and reality. The trick is to bring these two leadership styles and planning processes together. A strategic plan without supporting resources won't go far, and a budget without an underlying vision will stagnate. An institution that can pair strategic planning with strategic budgeting, on the other hand, will be set up for success.

Why Strategic Plans Fail

If you'd like to go through an interesting exercise, try to find older strategic plans for your institution. I did this once as I was organizing old files and was surprised that the strategic plans from ten or even twenty years prior didn't look very different from the plan created five years earlier. Not everything was the same of course, but there were a number of objectives and initiatives that had a strong similarity to current planning. There was a certain reassurance in this—the mission and vision of the institution had remained consistent over time. Yet it also meant that, even decades later, the museum was still having trouble achieving some of them. I don't think that's unusual at all. In fact, fully implementing a strategic plan is probably the exception. The landfills (and shared drives) of the world are littered with strategic plans that have failed and faded into irrelevance.

One reason strategic planning fails is that organizations aren't aligned behind the plan. Changing the status quo takes enormous commitment and energy. Every part of the organization and every other planning process needs to call back to and support the achievement of the strategic plan. Even staffing and budgeting need to align behind the plan in order to make it successful. For-profit businesses tend to understand this because their financial success hinges on whether they can successfully implement change. They won't stay in business if their plans aren't taken seriously. They'll invest time and money into making sure processes are efficiently directed toward their highest priorities. Yet museums and other nonprofits still struggle with successful strategic planning. Too often, instead of circling back, they just create another strategic plan if the old one fails.

Instead of creating another strategic plan, we might be better served to focus on implementation. Once a plan is created, how are we ensuring it will guide the organization? Are we truly investing in the strategic plan to help it succeed? Do staff members and stakeholders really believe in the plan? Improving implementation isn't easy, but we can begin by looking at the supporting processes of the organization. One approach is to make budgeting and the management of other resources a fundamental part of the strategic planning process. The budgeting process itself can support strategic planning by providing a more regular interval for check-ins and discussion.

Bringing Budgeting into Strategic Planning

You can create the world's most aspirational plan, but it's really just words on a page if you can't underpin it with the right resources. Money is the engine behind the ideas. This is why we use the phrase "put your money where your mouth is." In order to be successful, a strategic plan must be grounded in a realistic assessment of resources, both staffing and financial. Elevate budget and resource management to more than a few words on a strategic planning template. A potential approach would be to set up a second planning session for resource allocation, which would review each initiative and assign very concrete financial and staffing resources. This might serve as a second review, catching some of those initiatives that came out of an optimistic planning session but are not immediately achievable or sustainable for the institution. In my experience, we usually come out of a planning session with too many ideas. It can also help you refine priorities. If you realize that your initiatives are too ambitious, or that you have too many, can you pull back and identify where you should put your focus? Are there small steps you can take to get closer to your goals? Is your plan loaded too heavily on the first year or two?

Incorporating this type of review will also ensure that you bring the rest of the staff along for the ride. If staff members have started to dread or resist strategic planning, it may be because the planning sessions just result in more work that begins to feel unsustainable over time. Making sure that the plan is assessed and supported by real-world resources can help people remain excited and optimistic about the strategic direction of the museum. Give them a voice in choosing initiatives and in providing honest feedback on whether they're achievable with your current capacity. This will help protect your *most* precious resource, the goodwill, energy, and talent of your staff. Again, alignment is key, and giving people the space to really focus on strategic initiatives will set them up for success. If people are asked to do more than they can handle, they'll drop something (usually the new things once the reporting requirements drop off) or they'll get frustrated and eventually take their talent to a different institution.

This approach also helps distribute ownership of and accountability for the strategic plan. One of the common reasons that plans get set aside is that they "belonged" to a director or other senior leader who has transitioned out of the organization. If the senior managers, such as those directing the budget, also feel a sense of ownership and responsibility, they can help champion and create continuity for the planning objectives.

Bringing Strategic Planning into Budgeting

The other way to keep strategic planning and budgeting aligned is to go the other direction and bring the strategic plan into the annual budgeting process. Once you have a sustainable strategic plan, then it can become an integral part of the budgeting process. When you first discuss the budget priorities for the year, they should be reviewed against the strategic plan. Can you see the strategic plan reflected in the budget? Have you entered a new phase in the strategic plan that requires adjustment to the budget? If you did allocate resources in the budget previously, were they used effectively to further the plan? Was the budget and staffing plan realistic? This is also a good chance to review the strategic plan with staff members on a regular interval. We don't do this often enough. It's as if we believe the strategic plan will just naturally seep into everything we do. Budgeting is useful here because it offers a built-in interval (annually, quarterly) for reflection on the plan. Does everyone understand and agree about the direction of the institution? Or are individual or section priorities starting to drift away? All of these questions might provide insight into whether the strategic plan and strategic budget are supporting, or working against, each other. First, ground the strategic plan in a commitment of realistic resources, and *then* check the budget to make sure it's supporting the plan.

Just as a budget can bring a disciplined approach to planning, keeping it realistic and attainable, a strategic plan can also bring discipline to a budget. One of the challenges with budgeting is that things change throughout the year. In some cases, this is unforeseeable or due to a new opportunity that didn't exist when the budget was made. If agility is important and has been accommodated in the budgeting style, we might have allowed for this. At other times, this is because the planning for the year was sketchy or poorly defined. Or initiatives are reactive rather than proactive. Someone else presents an opportunity and we take it, easily forgetting to decide whether it furthers the strategic plan. If you're constantly making budget updates because of changing plans (not just changing circumstances), then your strategic direction might be unclear. You might be jumping at every opportunity or allowing yourself to be distracted by activities outside of your core mission and vision. There's a fine line between these two things, but constant course change can be disruptive to an institution. It will also make it nearly impossible to budget accurately and effectively, which undermines the process and erodes confidence in the budgeting process. Using the strategic plan to frame budget decisions and expenses can help keep things on track.

Opportunities

Overlooking opportunity cost is a common pitfall in strategic planning. Both strategic planning and budgeting should also include a discussion of what you'll no longer do or will phase out for the future. Too often, strategic plans are just "more and more," and they never include "less and less." This is another reason strategic plans fail. Some institutions might find it helpful to frame planning as a "some in, some out" approach, where no new initiatives are added unless others are removed. Or it could include a focus on efficiency, what existing processes you can automate or make more efficient so that you can better focus on your more strategic initiatives. It might also mean some initiatives are about how to bring in more resources (not just spend them). Incorporating a real discussion of resources isn't necessarily easy to do, but framing strategic planning in this way will ensure a more successful outcome. Grounding the process in a realistic and *disciplined* assessment of resources is a key to success.

One way to assess the true cost of an initiative is to understand the *opportunity* cost of decisions that are being made. In economics, opportunity cost is part of the equation when deciding on a new initiative or assessing the true cost of a current activity. It goes beyond the actual financial, or even staffing, cost to consider what is being *given up* in order to pursue that particular direction. You can think of it as the loss or benefit that's incurred because another option was chosen.

The idea of opportunity cost may be easiest to see in personal choices. For example, if you go to a concert on a Friday night, part of the opportunity cost includes the movie that you couldn't attend. Perhaps you would have enjoyed the movie more, so there is an opportunity cost if you attend the concert instead. Opportunity cost might also include the difference in ticket prices between the two events. This applies to major life decisions too. If you major in art history, you might not be able to study economics. Those of us in the museum field might recognize that a career in museums comes with an opportunity cost for not choosing a more financially profitable field. Yet, pursuing a more lucrative field would carry its own opportunity cost, the loss of satisfaction and meaning that we might enjoy in our current positions. The idea of opportunity cost is that every choice also includes a loss or benefit from the other options not taken. Opportunity cost is primarily financial but can also include non-financial factors such as time or enjoyment. It helps us remember the context and consequences around decisions.

In our own work, we can also consider the opportunity costs of strategic and budgeting decisions. For example, a museum may have to consider whether to implement a space rental program for weddings. The museum has to assess all kinds of factors—the staffing costs, the wear and tear on the facility, the expenses, and, of course, the revenue from the program. Those are standard factors. When looking at only the numbers, the museum may conclude that the program will be profitable so they should pursue it. But a museum may also want to review the *opportunity* cost involved in the decision. If they choose to create a rental program, they may be giving up some measure of public accessibility to the space. Or, by supporting a rental program, they may be focusing staff and resources on an area that's not particularly aligned with their strategic initiatives. Even if new positions will be created to manage the program, there's a tremendous amount of work involved for existing staff members in setting up and coordinating a new program. That might be time and energy best spent elsewhere. Or it might not. There may be an opportunity cost for maintaining the status quo and *not* having rentals. The museum may be giving up revenue that could support programmatic activities. Letting the space sit empty also has a cost. Or the museum may determine that hosting weddings has an opportunity cost because it will not be able to offer the space at a lower cost to student groups or nonprofits.

We assess opportunity cost all of the time without measuring it so concretely. In economic terms, an opportunity cost can be a very real financial measure. In museums, this is usually more nuanced. However, every time you select a goal and initiative, it means you're giving up something else. This isn't a 1:1 trade-off, necessarily, but choosing one path precludes others. During strategic planning and budgeting, we might include a discussion of the things that we will have to *give up* in order to accomplish our highest priorities. This includes financial resources such as funding, but it also includes more valuable resources such as staff time, focus, and energy. This again requires a disciplined approach. Otherwise, you might be tempted to attend the concert and then rush across town to attend the movie. You might feel like you're having a full, enjoyable evening, but find that by the end you're worn out and didn't truly invest in either experience. Or maybe you love every minute but blow your entire budget for the rest of the month. This is what institutional planning can feel like when we rush around trying to do too much. If you consider a typical strategic planning session, you might find that it glosses over the opportunity costs involved in the decisions. We usually choose too many initiatives and overlook the trade-offs they require. Particularly because we work in a field with limited resources and strained capacity, we can benefit from incorporating opportunity costs into strategic decisions.

When it comes to opportunity costs, strategic planning and budgeting can again complement each other. By using strategic planning as a check on our budget process, we can recognize that not all initiatives can be funded. We can bring our focus back to the institution's highest priorities. Incorporating opportunity cost will help us recognize that there are consequences when we don't manage the budget effectively, or fund things that are not part of the strategic plan.

Budgeting can also create a window into understanding the opportunity cost in the choices the institution is making. Budgets are quantitative, so it's relatively easy to see that financial resources aren't infinite. Your board or your creditors will remind you of this if you push it too far. You might see a very real deficit in your budget if you overextend your institution financially. Yet, we don't necessarily have a quantifiable measure to determine whether staff are being pushed too far, or organization capacity is being exceeded. People might get caught up in the moment or feel that they have no choice. So, budgeting can offer you a check on whether initiatives are realistic. It's a canary in a coal mine, so to speak. If your budget is constantly strained or there's never enough funding, it may also indicate that your other resources are stressed. It would be unlikely that your staff members have high morale, feel deeply satisfied and valued, and are aligned behind a vision, while the budget is a disaster. There's a correlation that can help point to higher truths about your organization.

Budgeting and strategic planning are linked, but all too often they're siloed in museum operations. By bringing these two processes back together, while respecting their unique nature, we can create a more aligned and effective long-term planning process. The processes can also support and put healthy checks on one another, reminding us to assess and understand the trade-offs for the decisions we're making as an institution.

Three Ways to Expand Your Financial Knowledge:

1. Find an older strategic plan for your institution. Do the objectives look familiar? How many of the initiatives did the museum achieve or complete?
2. Look over a recent budget and see if you can find tangible evidence of your strategic initiatives.
3. Look at your most recent strategic plan and review the resource allocation. Was it realistic and enough support for what you had hoped to achieve?

II

✠

CREATING BUDGETS

4

✦

Budgeting for Projects, Sections, and Departments

The best way to learn about budgeting is to just to jump in and create one. You'll begin with a small project budget, which will help you get used to the basic concepts, gain confidence, and demystify the process. Then you can expand into setting up and managing a larger section or department budget. Pretty soon, you'll be able to manage a budget of a small institution. Easy peasy. All budgets share commonalities, so the skills you develop will carry over to budgets of all sizes and complexities. As you'll see, the most important part of a budget isn't actually the numbers. It's the planning and preparation that goes into creating projections, deciding how to organize information, and knowing when to communicate with others about your plans.

Budgeting Software

There are many budgeting software products available, but I recommend using a spreadsheet program such as Microsoft Excel. If you don't have Excel, there are open-source options with similar features. You won't be using complicated features or formulas. You should be able to, for example, calculate a column of numbers using the sum feature and subtract one cell from another. If you don't use Excel or need a refresher, there are a number of free tutorials online. And if that's a barrier, don't worry about it. You can budget using a text program, and you can budget just as well with a pen and paper, and an online calculator. You can even budget on a cocktail napkin. A complicated software program isn't going to make you a better budgeter. If your goal is to become more proficient with budgeting, then increasing your knowledge and skill level with a spreadsheet program is a potential area for growth. But it isn't necessary to start.

Creating a Project Budget

A project budget is often used as a standalone grant or funding proposal budget. Or it may be for a specific project or program that you manage. For example, you may create a project budget to estimate the cost for re-housing a segment of the permanent collection. Or it may be for a specific public program that you are planning. Project budgets are generally concise and easy to manage, because the scope is limited. They can be a helpful way to learn the basics of budgeting.

As you start to plan your budget, you'll want to clearly identify the activities it supports and the time horizon. Is the project a one-time event or within a limited timeline? Or is it for all activities related to that project within a particular time period, such as a calendar year? Sometimes, it's also helpful to identify what the project budget *doesn't* support (for example, closely related activities that are within a different budget). Keep this scope in mind so that you budget for the correct activities and time frame.

Finally, you'll want to consider your available funding. Often for project budgets, the expenses themselves form the basis of the approved or requested funding. You might be submitting the budget as part of a grant request, or for approval from museum leadership. In that case, your budget request may be approved as written. In other cases, your funding will be more limited and you will be budgeting against a fixed amount. If you already know the amount of available funding, you can plan against it and build up expenses within the allocated amount. Knowing this in advance will save time and allow you to prioritize activities.

Planning Expenses

Once you've spent some time on preparation by determining the scope, timeline, and funding you can begin to create some expense projections. Begin by listing out the activities and expenses as well as you can. At this stage, you don't need to worry about being neat or thinking through the categories too clearly. You might find that some expenses are highly detailed, while others are fairly vague. Just starting listing and see where you end up.

Once you have a working list of expenses, go back and dig a little deeper. Challenge your planning to see if you can discover the assumptions beneath them. For example, if you're planning for a public program, did you make an assumption about how many people would attend? What is that assumption based on and how confident do you feel about it? Review your list to see if you can identify any associated expenses that you overlooked. For example, if you're going to mail event invitations, are you considering postage? If there are unknowns about the project, for example, an activity that you may or may not include, you can list those too. If you don't know the amounts, list the item as a placeholder for now. Table 4.1 shows what your budget might look like at this stage.

Table 4.1.

Saturday Public Program
Initial Planning Budget

Markers	$65	
Sketchpads	$200	
Stickers	$30	- rough estimate
Invitations (or just use social media?)	$500–700	- no idea of this cost, follow up with marketing
Artist honorarium	$300	- fixed, standard fee
Musical group honorarium	$400	- fixed, standard fee
Student staffing	$110	- calculated as 2 students at $11/hour for 5 hours each

I also like to use "breadcrumbs" when I create a budget. I leave myself all kinds of notes and information on the spreadsheet. You can do this right on the budget spreadsheet, or you can create a separate tab for your notes. This can include how you calculated an amount, where you obtained an estimate, the unknowns about your budget, contract terms, or things you still want to research. Don't worry about being messy, you'll clean it up later or you can always create a clean version if you need to share your budget. When you come back to your budget in three or six months, you'll be grateful that you left yourself notes to follow. If anyone else needs to pick up your budget, they'll be grateful too. It's also a good idea to store any relevant correspondence such as emails, vendor quotes, or price sheets in the same place as the budget document.

Categorizing and Confirming Expenses

Now that you have a starting point, you can begin to shape the information into a manageable and concise budget. One way to create structure is to categorize your expenses. You can leave them as a detailed list, but this isn't very efficient for budget management. For example, for a small education program, you might know very specific expenses, such as the cost of markers and drawing paper. Instead of listing each one on the actual budget document, I recommend combining them into a budget category such as "supplies." In most cases, it's beneficial to "zoom out" rather than "zoom in." You still might need to start with a detailed list in order to arrive at the larger figure. But then you can zoom back out to create a broad category rather than individual expenses. This approach also gives you flexibility. If the markers are a little higher than estimated, and the stickers are a little less, you don't have to reconcile each purchase against each individual budgeted amount. Table 4.2 shows how you might simplify your budget and categorize expenses into larger buckets.

Table 4.2.

Saturday Public Program (2/19/2022)
Planning Budget with Expense Categories

Supplies	$300	
Invitations	$500	- no idea of this cost, follow up with marketing
Honoraria	$700	
Student staffing	$110	- calculated as 2 students at $11/hour for 5 hours each
Total	**$1,610**	

While this might not seem necessary for a small budget, using broad budget categories will become useful when you manage larger budgets. It's easy to track two small supply purchases on a project budget. But imagine if you were managing two hundred supply purchases on a larger department or institutional budget. You would not want to maintain a list of two hundred separate purchases and then check off each one as you go. When you create a budget, you will eventually have to track against it, so using budget categories makes the process easier and more efficient. Categories also make it easier to create financial reports and communicate across the organization.

Once you spend some time categorizing and organizing expenses, you should have a working budget for your project. You'll then want to compare those projected expenses to the available funding (if your project has a fixed amount). In our example, we'll assume that we've been authorized to spend $2,000 out of the public program budget. At $1,610, we're well under this number. But a careful look at your planning budget might alert you to the fact that the cost of the invitations is a wild guess. This category needs more research before the budget can be finalized. You can see that underestimating on a small item like markers or stickers carries relatively little risk. If you're 20 percent off on estimating a $30 expense, it's only $6. Even being 50 percent off is only $15. But, being 20 percent off on a $500 expense is $100. Being 50 percent off is $250 more than expected. This can make a difference when the overall budget is only $2,000. So, on this particular budget, the cost of the invitations is the biggest unknown and, therefore, the biggest risk, so it's where you should put your focus.

To get a better handle on expense projections, you might talk to people who have experience in this area, check with a vendor, or look at past programs that also used invitations. Here, we have confirmed the cost of the invitations by talking with someone from the marketing department. They indicated that the costs had gone up and the invitations were likely to be $650. This was a little higher than we expected but is still well within the available budget. And by researching this expense more thoroughly, we've reduced the risk that the project will go significantly over budget. See table 4.3 for an example of how our budget might look when it's complete. This budget is ready to go and could be submitted as a supporting budget document to a grant or internal proposal.

Table 4.3.

Saturday Public Program (2/19/2022)
Completed Planning Budget

	Budgeted
Supplies	$300
Invitations	$650
Honoraria	$700
Student staffing	$110
Total	**$1,760**

Balancing Your Budget

If you do have a fixed budget and instead find that your projected expenses are higher than your available budget, then you'll need to find ways to do one of two things: decrease expenses or increase revenue. Those are the only two ways to balance a budget. For small project budgets, it's easiest to reduce expenses. On our sample budget, for example, we might decide to market the event exclusively on social media, saving the cost of invitations. Or we might reduce the hands-on activities to save on supply costs. Maybe we can call around to local stores to see if someone would donate the supplies instead. Think of this like a mini exercise in strategic planning. If you can't increase your budget and have to prioritize your spending, what activities are essential and which ones are secondary? Are there core activities that have to occur to make the program worthwhile? Or are there other programs that you would give up in order to increase the budget for this one?

Understanding Contingencies

When you create a budget, building in a contingency is a useful method for flexibility. A contingency is a (typically small) budget cushion that provides protection against unexpected events or slight variances in estimates. This gives you a little leeway in your planning. For example, if your estimate is $389 for a particular expense, you can just round up to $400. Take care, however, not to build contingencies at multiple levels or go overboard, or you'll overestimate and end the year with too much money left on the table. For example, if your supply budget is rounded up generously, don't also add a contingency to the project budget itself. Contingencies are best built in at higher levels, such as the project, section, or department level, where they can absorb overages from any of the expense lines below it. Or you can use contingencies on the budget lines that are the hardest to predict. Determining the appropriate level and placement of contingency takes practice, but eventually you'll develop more confidence in your projections. For budgets at all levels, you'll also discover that you can't go too far off course if you have regular tracking and reviews in place.

Tracking Expenses

Once you have a finalized budget and the project is underway, you'll need to establish a method for tracking your expenses. Tracking is comparing your actual expenses to your budgeted amounts. There are a few ways to track. The most common is monitoring expenses during regular budget reviews. You would review expenses that have posted on your institution's financial system, and then compare them to your planning budget. If you don't have access to the financial system directly, then you may receive a financial report with this information. If you're really fortunate, the financial report might even provide detail about your project. This is most likely to occur if you're using a dedicated grant, for example, or a segregated funding source. More likely, however, your project will be part of a larger section or department budget and you'll have to determine which expenses belong to your project.

Another simple way to track expenses is to enter amounts yourself on your spreadsheet as you make purchases. Your existing budget spreadsheet can also serve as a tracking tool. Your initial budget will become your planned expenses, and then you can add a column for "actual" expenses. See an example in table 4.4. This is where you'll enter expenses as they post. Then, at the top of your new column, you'll enter your starting budget amount. As new expenses post, you'll deduct them from the starting budget. You can even set up a formula to do this automatically. At the bottom, you'll see a running update of the amount remaining in your budget.

Table 4.4.

Saturday Public Program (2/19/2022) Planning Budget with Tracking		
	Budgeted	Actual to Date
Starting Budget	**$1,760**	**$1,760**
Supplies	$300	$200
Invitations	$650	
Honoraria	$700	$300
Student staffing	$110	
Remaining Budget		**$1,260**

If you're tracking on your own, try to establish a consistent interval for when you'll enter expenses. For example, you could log the expense when you submit the invoice for payment or when you see the charge appear on your credit card. Just try to stay consistent, however, or it will become confusing as your budgets become more complex. There's a benefit to waiting until expenses actually clear on your institution's financial system or on your credit card statement, if possible. By waiting until they're finalized, you'll know the actual posting dates and can also verify that the expense was actually paid. For example, if you had budgeted $300 for an honorarium payment and mark it as cleared when you submitted the payment request, you'll assume it was paid. If the payment gets caught up somewhere during processing, you might not know. If, instead, you wait for it to "clear," then the payment cycle has been completed and you can be confident that the vendor was paid.

Establishing consistent techniques for when and how to track expenses may seem unnecessary with a small project budget but will be essential as your budgets become more complex. You also don't want to duplicate work. If your institution provides financial reports on a regular basis (with enough detail on transactions to be useful to you), teach yourself to rely on those for budget tracking, if possible. For example, you would go through the transactions on the financial report, identify the expenses that are part of your project, and enter them on the spreadsheet. This will keep your budget review in cadence with the remainder of your institution and also help you get in the habit of regular and consistent review.

Whatever method you use to track expenses, you'll need to reconcile them against the planning budget at some point in the project. For a small project, you might just wait until the end and enter or verify all expenses. This is a good method if most expenses are predictable or you're not too concerned about going over budget. For a larger project, or one spread out over time, you'll want to reconcile expenses periodically to make sure you're on track. You might choose to do this quarterly or monthly, or when your institution does regular budget reviews. For some projects, you might discover that you need to make changes to keep the budget on track. For example, if a particular expense is much higher than you expected, you may need to find a way to pull back on other categories if possible. If you can't pull back, then you'll need to determine how far over the budget it will be and make plans for how to handle the overage. In either case, recognizing problems early will give you more time to adjust. You don't want to discover significant discrepancies when the project is over. Budget management often requires a proactive approach to prevent unexpected overages. Tracking is just as important as budgeting, so don't neglect this step.

Conducting regular tracking and reviews of your budget is also a great way to become better at budgeting. You might find that your estimates were way off, or that they were perfectly accurate. Once the project is complete, you'll want to take some additional time to close out the budget and assess your overall planning process. How did your total expenses compare to the amounts you budgeted? Did the categories you used work well, creating accuracy without taking too much time? Were they too detailed, or not detailed enough? If there were any estimates on your budget, how did they turn out and can you use some of that experience for the next project? Taking time to evaluate a project budget can provide meaningful insight into your budgeting style and help you build your skills. The next time you set up a budget for a similar program or project, you'll be even better at it.

Finally, before closing out the project, make any final notes and archive your budget in some sort of organized way. Your institution might have record retention requirements, which requires storage of this information for a specific number of years. More importantly, however, you may want to refer to your budget again in the future to help inform your planning assumptions. And then, don't forget to take a moment to congratulate yourself on successfully creating and managing a budget.

Section Budgeting

If you can create and manage a project budget, it's not difficult to roll that planning up into a section or department budget. This type of budget would represent activities associated with a particular section or department of a museum, such as education, marketing, or administration. Budgets at this level are slightly more complex, because they capture a variety of activities and programs and are often budgets for a longer time period, such as a full year. But even so, the basic concepts of how to set up and manage a budget hold true at all levels. In some sense, a section or departmental budget is built up from project budgets for various activities or programs. And then section or departmental budgets form the basis for the institutional budget itself. Building from the ground up makes a large budget more manageable to create and understand.

Establishing Section Budget Categories

As you create your section budget, you'll first begin to identify programs and activities that will form the building blocks of your budget projection. These are essentially line items within your budget. You should again take time to think through the best way to categorize the expenses you're managing. When you set up your budget, try to think ahead to how you'll manage the budget as the year progresses. It's relatively easy to create a detailed budget, but it's not easy to track against one. Keep your budget in perspective and spend time where it matters. I recommend only categorizing down to the level that will actually be meaningful to you and your institution. This might be based on broad categories used consistently at your organization, or categories used on your financial report. You might have obligations to funding agencies or report information to professional organizations. And the categories they use might be enough for your internal purposes. More likely, however, you'll need to create some additional subcategories specific to your section or department. Those categories might align with the section's major activities or subsection. Here are a few methods for establishing budget categories at the section or department level:

> *Categorize by specific activity or program.* You might, for example, choose to include a budget category for a single public program series, combining supplies, services, and even staffing in that one line (or in sublines, but all assigned to that particular program). Or you could create a line for a specific function, such as conservation in the curatorial budget. Budgeting by specific *activity* gives you an easy way to see the total cost for that particular program. This may be useful if you use a specific funding source, or if you need to analyze or report the costs of that program or function individually.
>
> *Categorize by position.* A related method to budgeting by activity is to align budget categories with staff positions or subsections. The person making the purchase may be the person managing the budget. So, for example, in a curatorial budget, there may be a sub-budget that's managed by the registrar. That person will create this sub-budget and keep tabs on it as the year goes on. In order to create clarity around those numbers, these expenses will be

categorized and managed separately. These expenses might still be part of a larger section budget, such as the curatorial budget. Then information and planning would filter up and down through the section budget manager. For example, a chief curator might manage the overall curatorial budget but incorporate planning by the registrar and curators.

Categorize by type of expense. You might instead choose to budget by type of *expense*, instead of specific activity. With this method, you could have one budget line for supplies. All supply purchases for the curatorial section would be on one line, for example, whether those supplies were used by the registrar or by a curator. Budgeting by type of expense is generally the easiest method, because all purchases of that type will just fall on that one line. The drawback is that you're losing some detail. If someone asked you how much you spent on registrarial supplies, you would need to conduct additional analysis to pull out those expenses. This would also be more complicated if multiple people are involved in making purchases that fall into one big category. It's harder to create accountability if multiple people are accessing one budget.

Categorize by some combination of activity and type of expense. Here, you might itemize out larger expenses as well as select activities or programs. These will be expenses or activities that need closer analysis, have their own funding source, or may be reported separately. They also tend to be the ones more central to your mission (or they should be). After itemizing out these large expenses or specific activities, you can then lump the rest of your expenses into broader categories. For example, a curatorial section might have a large collection re-housing project which they want to itemize out because they want to report the cost to the board. This is also a project outside of their normal activity, so they would like to keep careful tabs on the budget. This project includes supply costs for archival boxes, temporary staffing, and a new laptop. So, it's itemized on the budget sheet as "collection re-housing project." But the section also has general day-to-day supply purchases that support various activities such as registration, preparation, and photography. While these specific activities could also be itemized out, the supply costs aren't that high and the section doesn't need to report on them. So, these supply purchases can just go under a single line of "curatorial supplies."

For sections and programs that make small miscellaneous purchases through the year, you can consider the use of a "monthly average" as a catch-all for these low-dollar expenses. This will help you avoid categorizing and monitoring expenses that are relatively inconsequential. A monthly average can be a mix of categories, such as small supply purchases, an inexpensive service, or a low-dollar subscription. You would only track the big expenses, and then the monthly average would be everything else. Your focus is then where it belongs, only on those large expenses, and the rest are just monitored loosely throughout the year. It takes a little practice and analysis to make an accurate projection for a monthly average, but it will pay off in the time you save going forward. You can build a short list to determine the types of things that will fall in this category, or you can look at a past year to determine how much is spent on these small, miscellaneous low-dollar purchases.

Building on Historical Information

In order to develop a section or department budget, you should first start with historical information about expenditures if you can access it. If your section has not been actively budgeting or there's been some staff transition in this position, you can start by pulling out a recent financial report, or a list of transactions for the past year or two. Where normally you would first create a planning budget, and then review the financial report that is based on it, here you're working in reverse. You'll create a forward-looking budget based on past expenses. This may be time-consuming, but you should go through and categorize every single transaction for your section according to the budget categories you intend to use. This process will give you a deep dive on your finances and also help you verify that you're not missing anything significant. Depending on the size and complexity of your section budget, you may wish to review transactions for several years to get a fuller picture. As you look over transactions, try to identify those which are outliers. These are often large expenses that you don't expect to see every year. For example, the section might have purchased a large equipment item that will last for a number of years. These large one-time expenses are distinct from routine, ongoing expenses, such as small supply orders or subscriptions. You'll want to be careful to base the budget projection on expenses that are likely to recur every year.

If you can't access expense transactions from previous years, then you may be able to find summary financial statements for the museum. These are often found in annual reports or bulletins. A financial report will at least tell you how much was expended for a particular section or department. This can be the basis of a section budget as long as the number is used with caution. You can't see any detail under this number, so you may not know if there are any large one-time projects or unusual expenses for that year.

Finally, if you're starting a new section budget or can't access historical information, you can create a budget from scratch based on projections and estimates. This is unlikely to be as accurate as one based on past spending, but can create the basis for future planning. If you have sufficient funding, you can also just go without a budget initially, and only track expenses for a quarter or for a year. This tracking can then create a foundation for a future budget.

Being Strategic with Section Budgeting

Once you have a working baseline budget number based on historical expenses or estimates, then you can move on to planning for the new fiscal year. For example, do you anticipate any new expenses for the coming year? Or will there be any significant reductions in any areas? Do you need additional resources to accomplish strategic initiatives? Has there been a change in direction for the section or the institution? When it comes to more practical matters, do you anticipate any large supply purchases or equipment replacement?

If you're managing a section budget, then chances are there are other people working in your section. In that case, you have to establish a method for how those individuals will contribute to and interact with the section budget. They might, for example, provide estimates for areas they oversee or submit their own program budget that filters up into the larger budget. You might set up a planning discussion to talk over the section budget. Individuals in the section might have their own initiatives or want to propose new projects for inclusion in the section budget. They could also have insights into the needs of the section. Or they may want to suggest opportunities, such as a collaborative community program that they'd like to participate in. This again is a strategic exercise, only this time at the section level. It gives you a chance to talk about the upcoming year as a section.

You can see that section budgeting is closely tied to section planning. It's different from project budgeting because the scope is less concrete and the planning may be more complex. It may require harder choices about priorities. It can also reveal the need to shore up planning. If you start the year and don't know how many exhibition openings you'll have, however, or what types of activities will be at the opening events, it will be more challenging to create an accurate budget projection. If your planning is solid, then budgeting will be relatively easy. If it isn't, the budgeting process can be a nudge to solidify planning for the year. Planning can become particularly challenging across sections and this is where institutional budgeting becomes a key driver of communication and collaboration.

Three Ways to Expand Your Financial Knowledge:

1. Find a completed, small project budget at your institution. Review how expenses are categorized and if the project stayed on budget.
2. Review the organizational chart for your organization. Does it mirror the section or departmental budgets? For example, if you have a curatorial section, do you also have a curatorial budget?
3. Find out what financial system your organization uses for reporting purposes.

5

+

Foundations of
Institutional Budgeting

Institutional budgeting requires significant planning, communication, and strategic decision making. This is where museums determine how resources should be distributed and which of its priorities will be funded for the year. Taking time to create the foundations for a successful budgeting process will make the process more meaningful and effective. An institutional budget is larger and more complex than a section budget but, again, it's just built up from blocks. By starting with projects or programs, you can build up to a section or department budget. With section or department budgets, you then build up to an institutional budget.

Establishing Section Budgets

To create an institutional budgeting process, the museum will first identify the major sections or blocks that will form the basis of the budget. They will often mirror the programmatic activities or the staffing organization of the museum itself. If you don't have this structure yet, I'd recommend just roughing it out to begin. As you start to analyze and sort expenses, the categories will become clearer. If you're starting from scratch or making major revisions, establishing section budget categories is a good discussion to have with senior staff members.

If you're setting up a new system or trying to get a better handle on the existing one, you'll encounter some challenges the first time around. You can expect a lot of discussion and even debate over where expenses belong. This process will also reveal some of the planning and communication challenges in your museum. For example, when an expense pops up and no one had planned for it in their section budget, you may realize that you have some work to do on communication and planning. It's essential, however, that *every single* expense is assigned to one of the major categories you've established. This will allow you to create clear and organized financial reports at the end of the year. It also gives you the most accurate picture of the museum's financial situation.

While every expense has to belong to a category, not every expense necessarily has to be assessed through the budgeting process. Budgeting isn't financial reporting, so it doesn't have to be comprehensive. So, you should only use it for areas where you actually need to plan and monitor expenses. For example, you may have non-discretionary expenses that occur every single year. They're predictable and you know where the revenue is coming from. These will appear on the financial report, and do belong to one of the budget categories, but may not need to be included in the budget planning and tracking. Or you may list them as a placeholder but spend minimal time checking in on them throughout the year. Another example of expenses that can be excluded are those provided by your parent organization that are not billed to the museum. While the value of these services might be captured on a financial report, they don't have to be included in the budget process. Budgeting should primarily focus on revenue and expenses that are discretionary and controllable. If you do choose to exclude expenses from the budgeting exercise, however, just be sure you're excluding both revenue and expense. And don't forget to incorporate them back in at the end of the year when you create a financial report.

When you establish sections and budget categories, also consider how your financial reporting will be used. If your institution is a member of a professional organization, you may report information to them using existing categories. While you may not wish to mirror those categories perfectly, you don't want to have to restructure all of your financial information for a report. There may be other considerations, as well. You might find that your board is particularly interested in certain activities and will want to see them broken out. Or funding in your institution might align well with particular categories. You can use whatever budget categories make sense for your institution. It really doesn't matter that much how you construct your categories as long as you have clarity about where expenses belong. Most small- to mid-sized museums will use some variation of the following broad categories:

Administration. This is a large category that includes expenses like office supplies and equipment, IT support and computer purchases, facility maintenance, and security. General office supplies are here, while specialized supplies (drop tags, archival boxes) would then be assigned to the appropriate section. Lighting is an interesting area for discussion. In our museum, specialized gallery lighting is under curatorial. Regular lighting in office areas is administration.

May include HR expenses, such as recruitment or job advertisements. The administration budget might contain subcategories such as retail or rental programs, or these may have their own category. For museums located under parent agencies, some of the administrative support might be provided indirectly. For example, a university might provide security or maintenance for a museum. These may be considered part of the administration budget, although not actively managed as part of the planning process.

Curatorial/Collections. This category includes expenses such as curatorial research support, collections management, and registration. Conservation may be included in this category as a line item or as a sub-budget. Some museums also include exhibition costs in this category, while smaller museums may establish a different budget category for exhibitions.

Education/Public Programming. This category covers expenses such as tour creation, workshop, and docent program support. It sometimes also includes exhibition openings and associated programming.

Marketing. The marketing category includes expenses such as advertisements and public relations, as well as the design and production of marketing material. It may also cover website design and updates, or those may fall under administration. This is an example of a category that needs careful sorting and discussion. For example, is an invitation for an exhibition opening part of the marketing or exhibition budget?

Exhibition. This category includes exhibition lease fees, installation costs, supplies, and gallery signage. Exhibitions drive expenses at many museums, so this category may or may not include related activities such as exhibition opening receptions. In our museum, the exhibition budget includes only specific costs such as exhibition lease fees.

Staff Travel and Professional Development. You may establish a standalone budget for these activities, or they may be sorted out to each section. I prefer to manage them centrally so that I can see a more strategic picture of what types of training and development are going on across the museum. It also creates greater efficiency, so that funds are used where most needed and requested. If you do manage them centrally, then you may want to establish a system to ensure equitable access to the funds. If you assign them to the sections, then you may want to monitor how actively they're being leveraged.

Salary/Staffing. This category covers expenses for permanent, temporary, and student salaries and closely related staffing costs. May also include fringe benefits if your institution pays them directly. Depending on your staffing and funding model, this category may or may not need active management. For example, if your parent agency provides funding for permanent staff salaries and you don't manage that funding line, then you don't need to include staffing in your budget exercise. Or you may only need to budget for temporary or student staffing. In some museums, staffing costs will be assigned and managed by section. For example, salaries for administrative staff may be a line item in the administration section budget. This creates easier reporting but also siloes these expenses so that you don't have a comprehensive view of staffing expenses across the institution.

Empowering Section Budget Managers

Once you have the "big buckets," you'll need to establish who is responsible for each section budget. In a small institution, one person might need to oversee several section budgets or even the entire thing. In larger institutions, you might have subsection budgets below these budgets. For example, in the curatorial budget, the registrar might be providing information for a standalone budget or particular line items. *One* person will need clear responsibility for each section budget, however, in order to create accountability and avoid miscommunication. It's also best not to rotate individuals frequently if you can help it. Budgeting proficiency is built up over time and designating one individual will improve the efficiency and clarity of the process.

You can think of a budget as a contract between the section budget manager and the institution and its leadership. It requires trust and accountability on both sides. Creating a budget is a commitment that the budget manager will use the funds responsibly. They also have an obligation to accomplish what they say they will with the resources they request (or do their best). It's also important that the institution puts trust in a budget manager and allows them to manage their allocated funds and teams independently and effectively. It should also provide enough funding so that sections can accomplish their strategic initiatives.

If section budget managers are going to effectively manage their budget, it's essential that they have actual control over expenses and appropriate oversight over their section activities. This doesn't necessarily mean formal supervisory authority but a clear designation as a section budget manager. You should be wary of accepting, or assigning, responsibility without authority. Delegating authority also means that once a budget is approved, the section budget manager should no longer need to seek internal approval to make purchases. This will, of course, vary by your institutional and parent agency policies. At my current institution, a budget manager can make or approve purchases up to $5,000 without additional internal approval, as long as it's compliant with their section budget. They're still responsible for adhering to purchasing policies, which have their own requirements. But they don't need to check with the director, or anyone else, since the section budget was already approved as part of the budget planning process. Why would we approve it again? Responsibility should align with level of authority. So, if your director is approving $100 purchases, it may indicate an issue (unless, of course, you have two staff members and the director is one of them!). Section budget managers may not be receiving the information they need to manage their budget effectively, or you may not have clearly outlined appropriate approval levels for purchases. If you can't trust someone to spend $100, then they probably shouldn't be managing a budget.

Along with this authority is the ability to reallocate as needed within the section budget. Once the budget amount is approved, the section manager can decide to make adjustments within their own budget as the year goes on. They may find that a particular activity needs to be put on the back burner, while another has become more important. They have complete discretion to reallocate funding, as long as their overall section budget remains within the approved limit. Obviously, their budget decisions should mirror the strategic direction of the museum but that's true of all decisions they make. This structure, by the way, makes my job easier. They have authority and responsibility within their area, and I can focus on the authority and responsibility within mine. I manage the institutional budget, so I review the section budgets as the building blocks of the larger budget. I don't manage budgets below this level, unless someone asks for help or wants to talk over an issue. Section budget managers know their section and their activities best.

With this system, you'll also need to be sure that other sections can't bill expenses against another section without a clear decision or approval process. For example, the curatorial section should not be able to arbitrarily decide on an expensive ad campaign for an upcoming exhibition. This expense would fall under marketing, so the decision must be made in conjunction with that section lead. Budgeting authority roughly mirrors section or program authority. It also facilitates necessary communication between sections and activities of the museum. If the left hand doesn't know what the right is doing, you'll see this appear during budget reviews. Those "orphan" expenses that no one wants to claim are a symptom that you have a communication breakdown.

Giving budget managers authority over their sections can be an adjustment for directors and senior leaders, who may want to move ahead with exciting new initiatives or ideas without fully considering the budget implications. They may care about financial sustainability, but may be more focused on the strategic opportunity than the numbers. By empowering section budget managers to voice budget concerns and get clarity from leadership about financial and planning priorities, they will be able to effectively manage their budgets (and not coincidentally, their sections). At our institution, we have established a "director's opportunity fund" for this reason. This is a pot of funding that can be assigned by the director throughout the year as opportunities come up. This protects the section budgets from unexpected overages but allows the director flexibility to fund new initiatives. An effective institutional budget is then built from the ground up with careful management and accountability at all levels. Each person has their appropriate level of responsibility, input, and authority.

Beginning the Planning

A helpful way to frame any budget-planning discussion is to put the numbers aside. Talk about the past year and what's coming for the future. Discuss any challenges the institution is facing. Try to air any fears or concerns about resources or ownership of activities. Then review the strategic plan and identify the next action steps on your most important objectives. Grounding your budget discussion in this way can give you a shared perspective, centered on the strategic plan of your institution.

One of the chicken-or-egg style dilemmas in creating a budget is whether to lead with the projected expenses or to lead with the projected revenue. Obviously, these two categories eventually need to mesh, but there's often discussion about which one should be constructed first. A colleague at the Portland Art Museum, Gareth Nevitt, says, "no money, no mission." This reflects a belief that the available funding must lead the budget process. In this view, it's pointless to budget for initiatives that can't be undertaken because there is no funding. Therefore, it's better to assess the available funding and then establish the initiatives it can support. Leading with revenue is particularly effective when revenue is highly variable. Funding might change dramatically from year to year, so there's no sense in detailing out expenses until the institution has a reasonable projection of how much will be available. Initiatives may be strategic and worthwhile, but it doesn't always mean that there's enough funding to support them.

In our institution, we have fairly stable funding and predictable core expenses, so we create revenue and expense projections as a parallel process. The section budget managers build their individual requests, while I work on projecting the revenue. Then we bring it all together. In a good year, the revenue is enough to support the projected expenses. At that point, there's not much more to do, assuming all initiatives are in line with the strategic plan and approved by the director. We focus our discussions on the plans and activities of each section and how they relate to institutional priorities. At other times, the projected revenue isn't enough to support all of the things we want to do. During those years, we identify which initiatives have to be put on the back burner. We can, of course, also discuss grant funding or other outside support, but those typically need to be planned far in advance. So, in a short-term budget situation, most of the conversation is about controlling expenses rather than increasing revenue.

If you have a smaller institution and budget, you can create an institutional budget collaboratively. Funding priorities can be established by the group, and the discretionary budget is slowly carved up by section. This method requires good communication and a sense of trust. It can create a competitive environment, and managers who are better at speaking up and advocating may overshadow those who are less assertive. On the other hand, it gives all senior staff members a sense of ownership and deeper understanding of the budget.

Distributing Resources

There are several ways to determine how to distribute funds across section budgets. Each has benefits and is effective in different situations. Institutional budget planning should carefully consider the strategic priorities for the overall museum, as well as the needs and priorities of the individual sections.

Base Budgets

This type of budget planning allocates a base budget for each section or activity. This is typically based on historical spending with increases for known projections. The section budget manager then knows exactly how much has been allocated and creates plans around available funding. An example is consistently allocating $100,000 for education. If the section wants to take on new initiatives, they need to manage them within existing funds, or identify new sources of funding such as grants. The advantage with this method is that the funding levels are consistent, so the section budget manager has a sense of what to expect for the coming year. It's also very easy to manage a budget at the institutional level with this method. If you budget $100,000 every year for education, you don't need to go through extensive planning or analysis. Most of the strategic planning is pushed down to the section level, where the $100,000 needs to be used for the section's highest priorities.

You can probably see the danger in this technique, however. Budgets can become rubber-stamped and the section's expenses may "magically" expand to use the available funding. After a number of years, you may not even know what the $100,000 figure is based on. Using a base budget can result in inefficiencies and a lack of funding for higher institutional priorities. While it works well for that section, it may not work as well from a strategic perspective. Some sections may have more funding than they really need, while others may be short. If this type of system is continued year after year without close examination, it will almost certainly create pockets of funding for outdated priorities, overspending, or programs that would benefit from closer examination. The amount may eventually become too low to support the true core mission-driven activities of the section. This will limit growth and development in the section.

Using base budgets can also cause the section budgets to get out of step with the institutional plan. While most budget managers are responsible and strategic, using a base budget encourages focus on their own section's initiatives. There wouldn't be built-in opportunities to discuss priorities with other section budget managers. So base budgeting would require careful communication to ensure that section initiatives are actually in line with the institution's priorities.

Zero-Based Budgets

Zero-based budgets are just the opposite of base budgets and are started from scratch each time. Instead of assuming a certain level of funding, a section manager would itemize or list all activities, providing an estimate and a justification for each. The manager might rely on historical data to create projections, but previous spending in itself is not a justification. They're instead making the case for each program or activity. This can be a way to tear your budget down to the floor in order to more carefully examine each category and expense. This approach requires a lot of communication about section activities and institutional priorities.

The major drawback to this method is that it's inefficient. In reality, some expenses do just need to carry over year to year and requiring justification every year would take time and effort. It might also be an empty exercise if you're not actually prepared to reduce budgets or implement changes. For that reason, I wouldn't recommend this technique every year, but it's a useful approach to implement periodically or in certain situations. This can be a useful method if you find that your budgeting process has become stagnant, for example, or if you're facing significant budget challenges and need very close management. I would also recommend this method if you're stepping into a leadership position and want to conduct a careful review of the institutional or section budget.

Hybrid Approach

This method would use the best aspects of both techniques: creating a standing base budget for routine expenses and using zero-based budgeting for more aspirational initiatives. An example would be to assign a starting budget of $100,000 to education. This amount covers expenses that have been verified as core activities. The section could then create a "wish list" of projects that they would like to propose for inclusion in the budget. The "wish lists" of each section are then reviewed together to determine which are the highest strategic priorities and which can be funded. The hybrid approach offers efficiency, because budgets aren't built from scratch every year, but also creates some opportunities to secure additional resources for aspirational initiatives. This is also a great approach to facilitate interesting planning discussions with senior staff members. Instead of getting mired down in discussions about routine expenses, the focus shifts to only those more aspirational and strategic initiatives.

While there are many methods for distributing resources across section budgets, all techniques require collaboration as well as strong leadership so that each budget supports and mirrors the section's strategic plan. Section budget managers should be empowered, but there must be a clear budget review and approval process. Otherwise, you may create a mishmash of individual and siloed priorities. Budgeting can have a democratic aspect, but it ultimately requires clear decision making. Getting out to the institutional level allows senior leadership to align the institutional budget to its highest strategic priorities.

Three Ways to Expand Your Financial Knowledge:

1. Review a recent annual report to understand how section or department budgets are structured at your institution.
2. Try to learn about purchasing policies at your institution. Is there a dollar amount threshold for when purchases require approval?
3. Talk to someone who manages a section or department budget at your institution, and learn how they approach planning and budget review.

6

✛

Building the Budget
Review Process

After creating a budget, it's important to implement reviews on a consistent interval. Tracking and analysis are critical parts of effective budget management. In fact, they might be the most important aspects. If you don't check in on your budget, there's little point to creating one in the first place. Reviews are really where you can get beyond the numbers and talk about the overall progress of initiatives. If you only talk about spreadsheets during a budget review, then you're missing some opportunities. If you build in enough time and let the process unfold, then budget reviews will often segue into larger planning discussions.

In some institutions, every budget review will be a full meeting with discussion and analysis. In others, budget managers or other stakeholders may receive a budget report that they review on their own. The interval used for reporting and analysis will also vary. It may be done monthly, quarterly, or at other points in time. A colleague, Gareth Nevitt, chief financial officer at the Portland Art Museum, said they use monthly reports, which is useful but, at times, misleading. He remarked that "a month is not a trend." Expenses aren't necessarily even across the year, so one month may present a distorted picture. On the other hand, looking at reports on a monthly basis ensures that the budget is always top-of-mind. Some of the factors in determining your review interval and style are the size of the budget, the stakeholders who need to review the reports, the work involved with compiling reports (and dedicated staffing for budget management), and your tolerance for overages.

Quarterly Reviews

In our institution, we use quarterly reviews. I like to review budgets on the quarter because it's enough time to have some perspective but not too long that problems go unrecognized before they can be corrected. I also prefer to meet in person every quarter, because it's a good chance to discuss developments that have occurred and any planning assumptions that have changed. For budget managers

49

who may not interact with their budget frequently, a quarterly review is also an opportunity to check back in before too much time has passed. Like most things with budgeting, the decision regarding frequency and format of budget reviews should be determined by your institutional culture and needs.

When you do plan to meet in person, I recommend getting reviews on calendars far in advance, especially if they involve senior staff members. It can get difficult to schedule a group, and once time passes, the budget review becomes less effective. It's also harder to make meaningful adjustments if too much time has passed. Bookmarking them on calendars also gives budget managers plenty of advance notice and creates a regular cadence of discussion and review. I also appreciate that standing appointments imply that budget meetings are a priority on everyone's calendar.

Quarterly reviews usually need a little prep time, so you might aim to hold them around the 15th of the month following the close of each quarter. So, if your fiscal year runs July 1 to June 30, your reviews would be held around October 15, January 15, April 15, and then July 15 to close out the year. You might also want to start to combine the planning for the following fiscal year into the cycle. So, the April 15 review could serve as an initial planning discussion about the following year. When conducting quarterly reviews, you'll start to recognize a pattern across the quarters:

First Quarter (Q1). The first quarter is a short review, and often very straightforward. Budgets are unlikely to change substantially in only a few months. You might even choose to skip the first review of the fiscal year, or just distribute a budget report, if little has changed.

Second Quarter (Q2). The second quarter is a critical review. If you only hold one meeting, make it this one. You're halfway through the year, so you should have a good handle on the plans for the second half of the year and the budget projections that support them. This is also a time to start reducing, or potentially expanding, section budgets and reallocating if needed. It's also a good opportunity to take a close look at the revenue projections to be sure they're on track.

Third Quarter (Q3). The third quarter is rounding toward home and should again be a fairly short review if you made appropriate adjustments during the second quarter. By third quarter, section budget managers need to make final determinations about what expenses are still going to be incurred for the year. This is also a convenient time to review any final fiscal year deadlines, for areas such as purchasing.

Fourth Quarter (Q4). The final review, or fourth quarter, is an important one. You'll be tempted to skip it, because the momentum of the next fiscal year will start to take over. Try to build in time for it, however, so that you have the chance to really analyze the year. The fourth review is when you see how you did. This final review then forms the basis for the fiscal year financial report if you create one. It may also be used to adjust the planning for the next fiscal year.

Preparing Budget Reports

Depending on the format of budget report you use, it's likely that some manual adjusting and sorting will be necessary. In government museums, in particular, you may be relying on a financial accounting system to review expenses. These types of systems will show expenses, and sometimes will also show loaded budgets, but they tend to have limited use for actual budgeting. In other words, a financial accounting system may not really show you the amount that was budgeted against the amount that was actually spent. As a result, you may need to export transactions out to a spreadsheet in order to create a budget report that's meaningful for your institution.

If you're using a variety of funds and they don't neatly map to activities (one fund supports one activity, a.k.a. budget bliss), someone will need to compile the transactions for each budget manager. For example, the education department of the museum may be funded by four or five different funds. This could include three separate gift funds, one endowment, and two to three grants. In many institutions, these are all separate funds, with separate codes. Some of these funds may also support other departments, such as curatorial, so you'll have a mixture of transactions within a single fund. So, unless you have an automated way to code expenses to each department, or unusually savvy budget managers, the transactions may have to be manually sorted out to each department or activity. This is also a good chance to eyeball the transactions for the quarter, catching errors such as transactions coded to the wrong funds or other billing problems.

Depending on your staffing structure and access to the financial system, you might prepare a polished budget report for each budget manager with all of their transactions categorized, or you might just provide their transactions for the appropriate quarter. They will then need to take responsibility for organizing and categorizing them according to their own section budget planning. This is a useful method because it creates a shared sense of responsibility and offers budget managers a chance to review their transactions in more detail. It also simplifies budgeting at the institutional level. It's enough to assign transactions to the departments, then the budget managers will conduct the detailed analyses.

Section Budget Manager Instructions

Prior to the budget meeting, each budget manager should spend some time with their budget so they can come prepared for a meaningful discussion. Preparation will vary by institution and according to the format of the budget report. In our institution, section budget reports are distributed at least a week before scheduled quarterly reviews. Section budget managers then review and prepare in the following way.

> *Review and organize transactions.* Depending on the number of transactions, they may need additional cleanup and organization. For example, some section budget managers find it helpful to sort by type of activity or description. They may want to create an additional column with a subcategory or notes.

There may also be some transactions that they don't immediately recognize or that need additional research.

Update the budget. Once the expenses are organized, the budget manager should determine where they were planned for in the budget. The expenses should then be totaled and deducted from that line-item budget (this may be automated or set up with formulas). For example, if an educator budgeted $2,500 for program supplies and spent $1,000, they should update these columns to show that $1,000 has been spent and $1,500 is still remaining. In our institution, we call these "future" and "past" expenses. Whatever format you use, you want to ensure that the budget manager can clearly see the available funding that remains for that particular activity.

Review your projection. If a deficit or significant surplus is projected, the budget manager will try to identify what has changed. They're asked to be prepared to talk about the causes and what adjustments might be necessary. They also double-check all of the budget estimates to verify that projections are still accurate. If not, they can make adjustments or bring notes to the review meeting for discussion.

Budget Review Meetings

If you choose to hold budget meetings, versus only distributing reports, you may wish to start the discussion by reviewing the major trends and updates for the institution. This is a good time, for example, to look at significant changes in planning assumptions. After that, each section budget manager should have some time to summarize their area and talk about what (if anything) has changed with their projections. Try to avoid the tendency to get into the weeds, such as discussing a $35 charge and which section should own it. This time is valuable, so make the most of it. If you add up the hourly salary of each person at the table, you might gain some perspective on the cost of the meeting. It's best to focus on large trends, major concerns, or issues that either demonstrate that the budget is on track, may be veering off course, or may impact other sections in some way. And often, the discussions won't be about numbers at all.

In a sense then, these meetings become strategic plan updates. Most of what we do is connected to the budget in some way. One section might provide an update about their programming schedule, noting that additional programs were added or deleted that may impact the budget. Another might provide an update about revenue, such as the annual appeal or the performance of the museum store.

I recommend having one person keep brief notes during these meetings in order to record decisions or things that need follow-up. I use a standard format and then store the notes with the budget documents for that quarter. This is a good way to document the discussion and also provide some gentle accountability for action items. It's surprising how much you can forget in only a quarter, so the notes will keep these issues documented. This can also serve as running documentation as you shape your budget process. For example, you might decide that event invitations should be budgeted within the marketing department. By recording this decision, you won't have to rehash it the next time it comes up.

Visualizing Progress

During quarterly reviews, I like to create a dashboard to show section budget managers what percentage of their budget they have used. Then, I code the percentage as green or yellow to quickly indicate whether things look good or need more analysis. For example, you would normally expect to see approximately 50 percent of the budget expended by the second quarter. If the section had spent only 25 percent, or 85 percent, it might indicate an issue. This method has to be used with some caution, because for some sections there is considerable discrepancy between quarters. Percentages are not always accurate indicators, but they can be useful where budgets are more or less evenly used throughout the year, or where large expenses can be easily identified. A percentage can also help a section budget manager to see where expense projections may have been over- or underestimated. For example, if expenses are more or less even throughout the year and the percentage is very low, then it may mean that program costs are lower than expected or that some activities are not occurring as planned.

I also like to use a dashboard because it gives a high-level overview of what's going on in the institutional budget. While the expenses of one section might be running too high, and another might be too low, the number that ultimately matters is the overall budget variance of the institution. If all sections are running high, then I might have to analyze the potential impact to the overall institution. I also use a dashboard to check in on other categories such as variable revenue, student staffing, or staff travel and development.

Financial Tune-ups

Quarterly budget reviews can also prompt regular financial tune-ups for the institution. This is the perfect time to check in on any financial issues, such as your temporary staffing budget, grant application or report deadlines, or the art acquisition budget. You might also verify fund balances or transfer funds from your supporting foundation, if applicable. Beyond budget discussions and review of individual sections, you can use the compiled budget information to take a larger view of your institutional budget to make sure it's on track.

These checks can also connect back to the budgets for the remaining fiscal year. For example, if you discover that revenue is well below projections, you might need to take the opportunity to pull back on spending as well. Budget reviews provide a regular interval for checking in on all things related to the financial condition of our organizations. It's difficult to get too far off course if you're conducting quarterly budget and financial reviews.

Accuracy and Adjustment

While we all wish we could be perfectly accurate with our budgets, they're dynamic planning documents. During the budget review, you might find that some adjustments need to be made to the amounts or assumptions. For example, a budget manager may decide that an initiative should be put on hold or that a new activity should be added. I often find that by the second or third quarter review, projections often need adjustment. This should be done carefully, because you don't want to adjust the budget for every small change. But if you recognize that a large program will be postponed, you will want to remove it from your budget. This will keep your projections as accurate as possible. Quarterly reviews are the perfect time to recognize these trends and make appropriate adjustments.

Even with quarterly reviews, it's likely that your section, or even your institution, will end the year with a slight variance between the budgeted and expended amount. This is often caused by a single category or expense that threw things off track. This is especially true if a planning assumption changed late in the year (a public program was added or deleted, an artwork needed conservation unexpectedly, an estimate was way off from the final cost, etc.). Unless, it's severe or widespread, this is a case where you'll benefit from taking a balanced approach. If you're driving in an ice storm, the biggest risk when sliding is that you'll overcorrect. Those of us in Wisconsin know that you should gently pump the brakes only once or twice, and then actually loosen up your grip on the wheel. You'll still slide and it'll be terrifying, but you'll usually be fine. This takes some practice and experience, but a lighter touch on correction can help avoid more serious consequences and crashes. This is true in budgeting as well. If you have a one-time overage and understand why it occurred, that might be the only action needed. If, however, you slide on the ice every time you drive, you might need some new tires or a driving class. Try to make adjustments in proportion to the issue.

That said, what is an acceptable budget variance? It varies by institution, but I would expect to see no more than a 5 to 10 percent variance on a budget. So, for a $100,000 budget, a range of $90,000 to $110,000 is reasonable if it includes a lot of expenses that are hard to predict. $95,000 to $105,000 is better. $99,000 to $101,000 is rock star budgeting. But the reason for the variance is more important than the percentage or the amount. If you can get to the "why," it will probably tell you more than the "how much." And, as always, it varies by institution. That level of budget variance might not be acceptable at all for your museum. As budgets get tighter, tolerances become smaller by necessity. The funding source makes a difference, too. Grants really have to be managed carefully and typically have no tolerance for overages at all. Communication is important when it comes to setting expectations. So, if you're managing a budget, it's a good idea just to ask. Is there room for variance? If so, how much?

There is no universal format or approach to budgeting that will work for every museum. Creating clear budget categories will help facilitate discussion and accountability. When you first set up an institutional budget, the tendency is to either gloss over the process or, on the other side of the spectrum, to spend too much time on details. The best approach to budgeting is to find a balance between tight management and a hands-off approach. A museum without a clear budget process will struggle, but one that is too tightly managed will need to make constant adjustments that are time-consuming and frustrating. There is such a thing as budgeting a museum into the ground. Creating a highly detailed process won't be sustainable for most staff members. Yet, it does require an investment of time and attention, in proportion to the benefit you receive. Finding that balance is an art, and it's one that you have to create at your own institution according to your priorities, staff capacity, and financial situation.

Three Ways to Expand Your Financial Knowledge:

1. Learn what type of year your museum uses for budgeting (fiscal or calendar) and the dates of the budget cycle.
2. Even if you don't manage a budget at your institution, ask to observe an upcoming budget meeting.
3. See if you can find a copy of an internal quarterly budget report for your institution to see how the information is presented.

III

CREATING UNDERSTANDING

7

✠

Learning the Lingo

One way to make budgeting more transparent and accessible is to become more comfortable and confident about the terminology. This chapter will provide you with working definitions and explanations of terms used in budgeting, accounting, and financial processing. You've probably heard some of these terms before but may be unclear on what they mean and how they're used. Even experienced individuals are sometimes a little murky about financial terms and concepts. Getting familiar with the vocabulary of budgeting and financial management will help to break down the gatekeeping and increase your understanding. When you have conversations about budgets, it will also help ensure that everyone involved is discussing the same things. Finally, and most importantly, dropping one or two of these terms into a conversation is a good chance to impress colleagues and board members at your next reception.

Time Horizons

In order to understand what a budget is planning for, or measuring, you'll need to understand what time period is captured. Budgets may be approached in a few different ways. They might be activity or project based, meaning when the project is done, the budget is closed out. They could be fund driven, meaning expenses are planned against a specific amount of available revenue. Most often, however, budgets are time based and use periods such as a fiscal or calendar year.

Fiscal Year

Many museums and nonprofits budget on a fiscal year basis. Unlike a calendar year, a fiscal year doesn't usually start in January. The fiscal year timeline will vary from organization to organization. Some state government fiscal years, for example, begin on July 1 and end on June 30. The US federal fiscal year starts on October 1 and runs to September 30 of the following year. In this format, the fiscal year is referred to as the *ending* year. For example, using a state fiscal year, July 1, 2020, through June 30, 2021, is called "fiscal year 2021." This is sometimes abbreviated, as FY21 or FY2021. This can become a little confusing, because at some points, you'll be in *calendar* year 2020 and fiscal year 2021. Once you start to get more proficient with budgeting, you'll get used to this convention. You may even find yourself thinking in fiscal years rather than calendar years!

If you work with government budgets in particular, you may also encounter a biennial budget. This is a two-year budget. For example, when large state budgets are planned, they may go through a biennial budget process. The naming convention here is a little different. You'll typically see this written as the "2019–2021 biennial." Using the state fiscal year format, this covers the time frame of July 1, 2019, through June 30, 2021. In other words, even though it's called the 2019–2021 biennial, this is fiscal year *2020* and fiscal year 2021. A biennial is usually a rolling time horizon, so it would be 2021–2023, 2023–2025. A biennial may start with either an odd or even year.

Calendar Year

Other institutions and supporting foundations may operate on a calendar year basis, January to December. This seems very straightforward, but these organizations often interact with entities using fiscal year calendars. So, for example, a museum may operate on a fiscal year calendar but their supporting foundation may report revenue on a calendar year basis. This can happen, for example, when the parent agencies or management policies of the two entities are different. So, the foundation may report that they brought in $500,000 in gifts in calendar year 2020. The museum, however, may report that they brought in $525,000 in gifts in FY20. The two figures are different because they use different time frames. As with all things in budgeting, this isn't a problem as long as everyone involved knows what the numbers represent. Of course, when it's possible to align time horizons for partner organizations, it makes budgeting and reporting more efficient.

Quarters

Quarters are the building blocks of fiscal and calendar years. You'll often conduct budget reviews or receive financial reports on a quarterly basis. Fiscal quarters are just what they sound like, three months of a fiscal year. On a July 1 through June 30 fiscal year calendar, the first fiscal quarter would be July 1 through September 30 (of the starting year). This is often written as Q1, Q2, and so on. So, Q1 FY2021 is July 1 through September 30, 2020. Calendar year quarters are easy to calculate; January through March is Q1 of a calendar year.

Thirteenth Month

While regular people believe there are only twelve months in a year, financial people know that there are actually thirteen. The thirteenth month is a final month for reconciling and posting expenses, and making any final adjustments to the year. For example, on a state fiscal year, which runs July 1 through June 30, the following July becomes the thirteenth month. As you close a fiscal year which ends on June 30, there may be a few expenses still filtering in or adjustments that need to be made. If you pay a bill near the crossover between fiscal years, you may even be able to choose which fiscal year to use. It's helpful to develop an awareness of when the fiscal year ends for your institution. When you start to manage budgets, you'll find that the timing of expenses and billing can make a difference in the accuracy of your budgeting. For example, if you incur an expense in May but the vendor doesn't bill until June, you may find that the expense actually posts in July, which may be the following fiscal year. This will vary depending on your institution's accounting method and policies.

Year End

Year end is when the transactions are finalized and the books are closed out, in order to end the year and start a new one. Unless otherwise stated, it means "fiscal year end." This tends to be a busy time, because there's a lot to do at the close of a quarter or year. If you need assistance with things like budgeting or have financial questions, it's wise to avoid these busy times if possible. For business activities such as retail operations, this is also when inventories are conducted so that a museum can accurately assess its assets and liabilities.

Budget Types

In addition to the time period it measures, a budget document captures different types of activities. The type of budget indicates which expenses you're tracking, as well as which ones you're excluding. In common language, we just use the term "budget," but it's incredibly important to understand *which* budget that means. Also, if you ever request or reference budget information, or compare one institution to another, you need to know which budget you're using. Budget documents and financial reports can be used to "slice and dice" numbers in many different ways. The way that a budget is presented and structured can make a big difference in the impression it creates of the museum's financial situation.

Operating Budget

When you create and manage a museum budget, you'll typically be dealing with an operating budget. This is just what it sounds like, a budget that includes operating expenses. At the institutional level, this will include, for example, salaries, supplies, and services associated with activities such as administration, curation, education, and marketing expenses. Most project, department, or section budgets are also operating budgets. Basically, an operating budget picks up all costs associated with the operation of the museum.

During planning exercises, discussions about the operating budget may focus on expenses that will vary year by year and that can be controlled. For example, if salaries are fixed and funded from a separate funding source, you may not need to spend time analyzing them. If, however, they vary a lot or rely on earned revenue, then they need to be more actively managed. All operating expenses will need to be included in financial reporting, but they may not be in the mix when working on active budget planning. An operating budget only includes operating expenses and doesn't typically include capital expenses or art acquisition expenses.

Capital Budget

A capital budget typically includes large items related to facility development or investment. These are expenses that are outside of the normal operating budget. You will most likely see a capital budget in the context of new construction or a major renovation. For example, if you build a new building, construction costs are capital expenses and planned within a capital budget. The distinction becomes less clear for smaller construction projects and building expenses. For example, if you renovate the staff kitchen, that's likely a capital expense. If you install a paper towel holder in the kitchen, that's probably an operating expense. The distinction isn't always perfectly clear. In general, a capital expense is an investment, such as the purchase of an asset with a long-term life. An operating cost, on the other hand, is something required for day-to-day operations. If you include capital expenses in your operating budget, it may skew your numbers and create an inaccurate perception of what it actually costs to run the museum. For this reason, it's a good idea to separate out capital expenses and establish a consistent internal method for defining them.

Acquisition Budget

One of the important distinctions about art museum budgets is that operating budgets are typically kept separate from acquisition budgets. Acquisitions refer to artwork and other items that are purchased for the permanent collection. It might also include closely related activities such as shipping those items to the museum. Acquisition purchases often use restricted funds and the acquisition budget can be quite high. As a result of purchases and donations, the permanent collection of a museum is typically very valuable. Museums, however, are guided by best practices in the field, which advise against treating the collection as a financial asset. It is protected and insured, but it is not monetized, in the sense of it being represented on a balance sheet (a listing of a company or institution's assets and liabilities). This is done for several reasons, but the most important one is that collections are not treated as financial assets that can be liquidated. This helps shield the collection from being sold to pay operating expenses. While creating a separate acquisition budget is common practice, it's not universal. In smaller institutions, acquisitions may be treated as part of the operating budget, especially if they're sporadic or low dollar. Again, consistency and clear communication are key.

Pro Forma Budget

This is a projected or planned budget. It's often used when a new program or change is being considered. For example, you might produce a pro forma budget when considering a new earned revenue program. The pro forma budget includes projected revenue and expenses, and only looks at the impact of that particular program. A pro forma budget is created in advance of committing to a new program or initiative, and becomes part of the decision-making process.

Overall Budget

This budget goes by various terms, but represents all revenue and expenses within the museum's budget. This is the "big bucket" representing the operating budget, the capital budget, and the acquisition budget. Outside of direct funding and expenses, the organization typically has a lot of discretion over what to include in their overall budget. For example, the overall budget of some museums might include in-kind support such as security or facilities services provided by a parent organization. Sometimes there are advantages to including everything possible in order to maximize the museum's stated budget. For example, a larger budget might mean that a museum is categorized with a different set of peers, which can help the museum make a case for more funding or a larger staff. When you see salary surveys, for example, museums are grouped by the size of their budget. At other times, there are advantages to only including the funding and revenue that are directly managed by the museum. For example, a lower budget may make the museum eligible for different types of funding. Because there are no hard-and-fast rules about what should be included in a museum budget, especially for institutions under a parent agency, it's open to some interpretation. As you can imagine, these decisions create very different pictures of funding models and expenses.

It can be really helpful to see the overall budget of a museum, but lumping everything together can also create misconceptions. For example, if the museum has restricted funds for acquisition, the overall budget may show a significant surplus. An overall budget is a bird's-eye view, so you'll lose some detail at this level. The overall budget will give you a sense of the scale of a museum's operation, but then it's usually necessary to dig deeper for a fuller understanding.

Budget Review and Reporting

An important part of budgeting is reviewing how expenses compare to planning. Unless you only have fixed expenses, it's hard to be perfectly accurate. This is part of the natural ebb and flow of budgeting. As you create and start to manage a budget, you'll use and see particular terms that refer to the accuracy and status of the budget. Understanding these terms will help you monitor and analyze your budget throughout the year.

Variance

A variance (or more accurately, planning variance) refers to the difference between what you planned and what you actually spent. Your institution may look at quarterly or monthly variances to give you a sense of how much was spent, or brought in, to date. A variance can refer to either revenue or expenses, but budget managers will usually be analyzing variances on the expense side.

Variances can be favorable or unfavorable. For example, if the education department had a $50,000 budget for the year, but spent $51,000, they have a $1,000 variance. Although this is a positive number, it's an *unfavorable* variance. They spent more than they had planned. If the education department had a $50,000 budget but only spent $30,000, they would have a negative $20,000 variance. This, however, would be a *favorable* variance (although their planning could use some work). If you get confused about whether a variance is favorable or unfavorable, just look at the budgeted amount and then look at how the expenses compare.

Variances can be calculated at different levels. They might be calculated on an individual expense, on expense categories, on section budgets, or on the institutional budget. Or they might be assessed at all levels, with variances rolling up to the larger budget. The decision of where to calculate and analyze the variance makes a big difference. For example, it's fairly significant if the curatorial budget has an unfavorable variance of $20,000 (overspending) and the education budget has a favorable variance of $20,000 (underspending). Those are both large variances relative to their budgeted amount. Yet, when looking at the institutional budget, the two variances balance out, leaving no variance at all.

To create an efficient, yet meaningful, budget review, you should consider how and when to measure variances and who is responsible for them. For example, at our institution, our budget process primarily focuses on variances at the section level and above. We don't typically discuss variances on individual expenses or expense categories, unless they're significant. A section budget manager manages variances below the section level. For example, if one expense category in their budget has an unfavorable variance, they might manage it by reallocating from other categories. These shifts are at their discretion, as long as they stay within the budgeted amount for the overall section.

Variances are a useful measure but also have to be viewed with caution. Few museum budgets are evenly distributed across the year. If you have a large expense post in the first few months, it may create the impression that the budget is overspent. Yet, the expenses may be low for the remainder of the year. Like most budgeting tools, a variance calculation is just an indicator and a prompt for discussion. Your goal is to be able to understand the reason for the variance and to determine if it's a cause for concern.

Surplus or Deficit

While a variance refers to a discrepancy in planning, a surplus or deficit refers to the overall impact on the financial situation itself. To understand a surplus or deficit, it might be helpful to think of your personal finances. If you had planned to spend $500 on groceries but actually spent $600, you have a positive (therefore unfavorable) variance. You spent more than you had planned. If you only had $500 total in the bank, then you also have a $100 deficit. You might have created an overdraft on your bank account. If you had a little leeway in your household budget, however, and actually had $600 available in the bank, you didn't create a deficit. It may mean, however, that you had to spend less on entertainment or had less to save. You might also be able to avoid a deficit by bringing in more money;

for example, you might sell a few things to cover the difference. So, a variance isn't quite the same thing as a surplus or deficit, but they're often related.

A surplus or deficit might even be predictable or planned. So, for example, if a museum has sufficient funding but doesn't spend all of it, they may create a surplus that rolls over to the following year. Determining whether a budget will create a surplus or deficit is the "bottom line" on a financial report, and a good indicator of how the museum is doing financially.

Surplus

A surplus is excess revenue or funding, after expenses are deducted or projected. For example, if you have $200,000 available and only spend $190,000, you have a surplus of $10,000. Or, if you have $200,000 to spend and project that you'll only spend $190,000, you have a *projected* surplus of $10,000. A projection may or may not turn out to be accurate.

A surplus is generally a good thing. A surplus can be misleading, however, if you're not accounting for fund restrictions. For example, some museums may have large endowments and large surpluses that carry over year to year. But funds may be heavily restricted and can't just be used for anything. So, not all surpluses are created equal. Many museums will carry over restricted funds from year to year. Looking at the surplus or deficit on unrestricted funds is a better indicator of their overall financial position.

Deficit

A deficit is the opposite of a surplus. In simple terms, a deficit is when there is not enough funding to support expenses. If you have $200,000 to spend and spend $210,000, you have a $10,000 deficit. A deficit is rarely a good thing, but it's helpful to understand the context around it. What is the deficit actually reflecting, and how big of a problem is it? There are two primary types of deficits: structural and cyclical.

Structural Deficit

This term is often used in the context of government or public budgets. A structural deficit is when the ongoing operational costs are *routinely* exceeding the ongoing revenue/funding. A structural deficit is often long-term and can usually be predicted. So, for example, a museum brings in $2,000,000 every year but expenses are totaling $2,100,000. This isn't because funding is lower than expected or because expenses were high for one particular year. It's a long-term issue of spending that exceeds revenue, even when times are good and projections are accurate. Often, these are issues that are hard to correct—such as pension fund obligations, real estate lease, debt repayment, or other expenses that can't just be cut. This is a difficult situation because, until it's corrected, the deficit will start to snowball on itself, becoming larger and larger each year. If an institution incurs a $100,000 deficit every year, within only ten years it will have a $1,000,000 deficit (not to mention the interest on the debt). You can see how quickly a structural deficit can get out of hand. So, in order to regain control, the museum would have to take care of the existing deficit *and* make changes so that it doesn't keep occurring. Usually, this takes time to reverse, and requires some combination of increasing revenue or funding and decreasing expenses.

You can recognize a structural deficit in a few places. If you pull the financial reports for a few years in a row, or the museum shows them side by side, you may see a pattern of running a deficit every year. That may point to a structural deficit. You may also see this in carryover deficits, if the museum reports them. Some annual reports will even be transparent about structural deficits and discuss the challenges they present.

Cyclical Deficit

A cyclical deficit is a more manageable situation. As a project or department budget manager, this is the type of deficit you're more likely to encounter. This tends to be a short-term situation and it may not be completely predictable. For example, a museum may bring in $2,000,000 and normally spend $2,000,000 (wow, impressive budgeting!). From year to year, they might have a very small surplus or deficit. This ebbs and flows and is usually manageable. But one year, something unexpected happens and they spend $2,200,000. This is a deficit and it's a concern, but it's not a structural deficit. The museum may be able to "tighten its belt" or do a one-time fundraising drive and get back to normal. Once this deficit is handled, there's no reason to believe it's going to come up every year. Distinguishing between the two types of deficits is helpful, so you can understand what caused the issue and how much course correction is needed. Tolerance for deficits (if any) will vary considerably by institution and by your particular policies.

Contingency

In budgeting, a contingency refers to building in a small "cushion" or extra revenue in case something unexpected happens. A good way to avoid a negative variance or a deficit is to build in a contingency. On large building projects, for example, you'll almost always see a contingency of 5 to 10 percent in the budget. In general, the larger and more complex the project, the more important it will be to build in a contingency. Using a contingency is a good approach for staying within the budget. The contingency gives you a little leeway for schedule delays, underestimates, supply problems, and so forth. Contingencies are a great tool when used thoughtfully and in moderation. If you use them too liberally, however, you're no longer building in a contingency, you're just inflating your budget.

Carry Over

Carry over typically refers to funds (but sometimes expenses) that will carry over from one fiscal year to the next. Some funds, such as gifts or endowment income, will carry over. Sometimes, however, a fund may not carry over. For example, if government funding is not spent within the designated fiscal year, it may "lapse" back to the parent agency. This is why you sometimes hear of government agencies scrambling to spend funds before the end of the fiscal year. Grant funding may or may not carry over.

Expenses and Revenue

Fixed Expenses

Fixed expenses are those costs that don't change from year to year. By their nature, they're regular and predictable. They can also be defined as expenses that will stay the same regardless of the level of service you're providing. For example, a lease cost or a service contract is a fixed expense. Assuming you stay in the same building, the lease cost will be the same whether you have ten thousand visitors or one hundred thousand visitors. Even fixed expenses change over time, however; you might not renew a lease, for example. Even so, fixed costs are relatively consistent over time.

Variable Expenses

Variable expenses are those that vary over time. They may be tied to some measure of performance or production. For example, if every visitor receives a $1 pin when they walk in the door, the $1 is a variable expense. If you have one hundred thousand visitors it will cost you $100,000. But if you have ten thousand visitors it will only cost you $10,000. A variable cost often scales up or down with the level of activity. The term "variable expense" can also be thought of as a cost you can control to some degree. You may decide to have fewer public programs, for example, which means a program is a variable expense.

Revenue and Funding

Both terms refer to money coming in or being earned. When you're speaking of overall revenue or funding for the entire museum, you can use them nearly interchangeably. For example, "How is our overall revenue looking for the year?" You could just as well say, "How is our overall funding looking for the year?" In common use, they essentially mean the same thing. There are differences, however, which are more apparent when looking at specific funding sources. The difference between income, revenue, and funding is kind of subtle and, like learning a language, you'll start to recognize which terms work with each other. The best clue is whether the funding source is earned actively (revenue) or received passively (funding). There are a few exceptions, but you'll generally use the terms correctly if you follow this guideline.

Revenue or Income

Revenue is income that you create or earn. So, we'll commonly refer to "earned revenue" or "endowment income." Revenue is typically "generated," so there's a sense of self-sufficiency implied in this term.

Funding

Funding is more often applied to money that's provided—university funding, government funding, grant funding, and the like. The same money can change as it filters down. For example, if a state government collects taxes, it would be "tax revenue." This is because they're generating or collecting it. If it then allocates some of this money to a state museum, it would become "state funding." This is because the museum is now receiving it from the state.

Gross Revenue

When discussing revenue within a budget, we usually mean "gross revenue," or revenue *before* expenses. So, for example, your museum store might generate a large amount of *gross* revenue each year. These are the sales coming in. Gross revenue doesn't account for the expenses going out, so it can be a misleading measure if not used carefully. Notice here that you wouldn't often use the term "gross funding." This is again because funding is usually received, not earned, so there aren't offsetting expenses.

Net Revenue

Net revenue, on the other hand, is revenue *after* expenses. So, while your museum store might generate a large amount of gross revenue each year, you might find that the *net* revenue is small. The store might need to cover the cost of salaries, goods sold in the store, and shipping costs. Net revenue is the more important measure, because it gives you a true sense of the revenue being generated after expenses. The relationship between gross and net revenue is important, because if you're only looking at the funding you're bringing in, you might come to an incorrect conclusion. Your museum store might have brought in more revenue than ever before this year! Wow, revenue is really up. But if the spending has crept even higher, the overall net revenue might not look so good. This idea is particularly important for programs that generate or run on their own revenue. For these programs, you'll always want to pair revenue with expenses so you can get an accurate picture of how they're actually doing. While it's true that it often takes money to make money, expenses have to be assessed in the context of the revenue they help create.

Financial Processing

Financial processing refers to activities such as invoice payment and fund management. While it's not the same as budgeting, you may encounter financial processing terms when you're managing a budget or reviewing a budget report. And as you become more engaged with budgeting, it's likely that you'll also have some responsibility for expense management and financial processing.

Encumbrance

If funds are encumbered, they're formally committed or reserved for a particular use or purchase. The funds have been allocated on a purchase order or some other mechanism (it's more than just "planning" to use funds a certain way). On financial reports, encumbered funds are treated much like expended funds since they're already allocated. Encumbered funds typically carry over across fiscal years, and you may have to "unencumber" funds to release them.

Purchase Order

Purchase orders are used most frequently by government museums. A purchase order is a tool that can "encumber" a certain level of funding. For example, if you have an exhibition contract with multiple payments, your institution may set up a purchase order for the full amount. You may also be required to set up a purchase order for routine purchases, such as a pest control contract or gallery lighting. Even though the payments won't be made for a while, the funds are "encumbered" and no longer available for other uses. You may also hear the term "requisition." They're often used interchangeably, but technically a requisition is a pending purchase order.

Cash Flow

Cash flow is actual cash going in and out. When using an accrual accounting system, cash flow will not be the same as the accounting entries. This can get complex, but accrual accounting is based on credits and debits, not in cash. For example, if the museum receives royalty payments from a publisher, they may record the earned royalty revenue before the cash payment is actually received. Don't worry too much about cash versus accrual accounting, unless you handle larger delayed payments or revenues.

Cash flow can also be a factor when it comes to the timing of expenses or revenue. For example, you might have a $100,000 annual budget for your section, but you might not actually start the year with that much revenue. So, you'll have to keep an eye on cash flow so that you don't spend money before you receive it. Sometimes institutions don't really have a budget problem, they have a cash flow problem. This is primarily an issue of timing. For example, if you receive your paycheck on the fifteenth of the month but your rent is due on the tenth, you may have a cash flow problem. You have enough money for the month, it's just that some expenses are due before your revenue is received. You know that you're going to get a paycheck, so it's not a problem, but you may have to float that expense or get one month ahead.

Financial Reporting

Museums use different types of financial reports to represent their financial activity and situation. While financial reports are clearly defined in the for-profit business world, they are used less consistently in museums and nonprofits. Even so, there are a few types of financial reports you can expect to see. Financial reports are always backward looking. Unlike budgets, they are reporting on what has already occurred, not what is planned or projected. For that reason, financial reports also strip away any kind of false optimism or spin that a museum might put on a budget planning document. If you want to know how the year *really* turned out, look at a financial report, not a budget.

Income Statement

An income statement shows high-level activity over a specific period of time, typically a year. The income statement will show revenue or funding coming in, such as sales/income, and expenses going out, such as cost of goods sold/supplies, tax, and other items. You may also see this document called a "statement of activities" or something similar. A budget attempts to project the income statement. The main thing to know about an income statement is that it shows activity for the year. It won't show, for example, the amount of debt or property owned by the organization. So, it can tell you how the organization did for that particular year (or quarter or biennial), but it doesn't show the overall financial situation.

Balance Sheet

A balance sheet, on the other hand, represents the organization's financial situation at a particular moment in time. A balance sheet is typically prepared at the end of the fiscal year. It lists assets and liabilities. For example, under assets it may show property, cash, equipment, and inventory. Under liabilities, it may show debt or unpaid invoices (accounts payable). It does not, however, show you activity over the course of time. So, you won't see categories such as revenue or expenses on a balance sheet. A balance sheet is useful because it's the best indicator of an organization's financial position. You might see it called a "statement of financial position," or a similar name. You might notice that the income statement is "active" (it captures activities and trends), while the balance sheet is static (it shows a position).

There is, of course, a relationship between the income statement (activity during the year) and the balance sheet (the financial position). If the museum spends more than it brings in, you will first see this reflected on the income statement. And it will likely filter over to the balance sheet, because the museum will have spent down some of its assets or acquired new debt. If a museum takes out a large loan, on the other hand, you won't see it directly on the income statement because debts aren't shown there. But you may notice more interest expense being paid in a particular year. So, there are connections between the two types of reports, but they represent different things.

Continuing to Develop Vocabulary

The above definitions are commonly used in museums and nonprofits, but there are often subtle differences in terminology. The best way to become familiar with the terms and documents used at your own museum is to look through the annual report and to sit in on budget meetings. Also, ask questions! You might be surprised to discover that you're not the only one who doesn't know the definition of the term being used. Being open about questions can help promote financial literacy across the organization and create productive discussions. You can also continue developing your knowledge by reading financial articles, particularly those about other museums or similar nonprofits. You will see many familiar terms and will often come across new concepts as well. By slowly building your vocabulary, you can build your own financial knowledge and confidence.

Three Ways to Expand Your Financial Knowledge:

1. Choose at least one financial term to learn about in more depth. Search for the term online, read related articles, and use it in a few sentences (even if you're talking to yourself).
2. Teach someone else about one of the concepts that's new to you.
3. Find an annual report for your museum (or another) and try to find these terms in the text.

8

Building Financial Literacy

If terminology is the vocabulary of budgeting, then literacy is the fluency. It represents ease and proficiency with larger concepts and more complex subjects. In order to have meaningful conversations about resource management, the people involved need to speak the same language and share a basic level of financial literacy. To create truly collaborative planning, budgeting has to engage staff members across the institution. Pushing financial information out to people is a one-sided conversation that doesn't invite them in or leverage their perspectives and expertise. Increasing the financial literacy of an organization takes time and patience, but it will pay off in greater contributions to the strategic direction of the institution. Financial literacy is not just a professional skill, either. Strengthening financial knowledge can also be a benefit in personal budget management, as well as a useful skill in volunteer and board positions.

First, Start at the Top

When building the financial literacy of an organization and creating a collaborative budgeting process, it's incredibly important to have sponsorship at the highest levels of your museum. This usually means the director but can also mean board members or department heads. I've implemented, or participated in, budgeting in a few different institutions, and sponsorship can make a big difference in engagement across the organization. For example, at one organization, the director didn't see the need for senior staff members to get involved with budgeting. He felt that the museum was in a good financial place and that involving other staff members would create inefficiency or even confusion. He wanted them to focus on their own areas of expertise. Not surprisingly, senior staff members were reluctant to take responsibility for budgeting. They weren't held accountable and didn't feel truly invited into the process, so they weren't engaged either. While the museum functioned relatively well, senior staff members didn't have a clear understanding of how priorities determined the distribution of resources. The situation eventually changed, but it was difficult to get traction, initially, without the director's endorsement. Trying to implement a new process without the full support of leadership led to conflicting messages and a lack of consistency about expectations.

At another institution, the director was a champion of the budget process and deeply believed in the importance of it. She considered it part of her responsibility to the institution. As a result, senior staff members went along for the ride willingly, and were also held accountable for their roles in the process. This director viewed financial literacy as a complement to each individual's own subject matter expertise. They were expected to be prepared for budget meetings, and their opinions and concerns were considered during the budget development process. They also learned a lot, not only about budgeting but also about how decisions were made. The process became much more collaborative and senior staff members contributed as fully engaged participants. It was also a messier process, because it took time to prepare reports, answer questions, and hold budget discussions. But the investment paid dividends.

I don't present these two scenarios as good or bad. Both leaders were thinking about the well-being of the institution, they just had different priorities and methods. But these examples help illustrate how the attitude of leadership will filter into the culture of the institution. One believed financial literacy was critical, which set an expectation for the museum staff. This is yet another example of how budgeting goes beyond the numbers. Everyone wants a financially sustainable museum. But not everyone agrees on how to get there. So, if you're planning and implementing a new budget process, or reinvigorating a stale one, start at the top. Your first job is to get the director on board. Some directors won't need convincing, but others may need to talk it through before they'll back the implementation of a new system. If you can't get the director (or other decision maker) to sign off, then proceed with caution. A large shift is unlikely to be successful and you might be better off making small, incremental changes. In all aspects of budgeting, it's important to take cues from leadership and build from a base of strong sponsorship. This will make your job easier and make implementation more successful.

And if you are the director or senior leader, be sure to demonstrate your own commitment to the process if you expect others to come along for the ride. You should be learning alongside the senior staff, encouraging questions, and finding opportunities to build knowledge across the organization. Even small gestures and reminders can convey your support for the process. If you're tasking someone else to implement change, set them up for success by visibly backing their efforts. This goes for any initiative but is especially true for areas like budgeting, where some staff members may feel that "it's not their job." Making financial literacy a small part of everyone's job not only establishes expectations, it demonstrates that you value transparency and input from across the organization.

Then, Build from the Ground Up

Once you have the endorsement of leadership, getting to the roots of an organization can be an effective way of actually implementing change. One of the best ways to develop financial literacy is to have people set up and manage budgets for their activities and departments. Responsibility should be proportionate to the position, of course. But even entry-level positions can, and should, have some responsibility for managing small project budgets. The best way to reach a leadership position with confidence about budgeting is to build the skillset throughout your career. So, if you don't already manage a budget of some sort, talk with your supervisor about ways you can get more involved.

If you're implementing a new process, it may be most effective to work one-on-one with people, or with small groups. Then you can come together as a larger group when the groundwork has already been set. This a good method for all topics where people may feel unsure or intimidated by the information being presented. Sharing financial information in large meetings can be overwhelming for people not proficient in budgeting. If they've seen it before, however, they'll come to a meeting with a base of understanding and have time to formulate thoughtful questions and comments. This also helps promote the idea that a budget is a two-way conversation, not just a document handed out at a staff meeting. Working with people individually will also clue you in to each individual's proficiency and confidence with budgeting. Some people will need more coaching, while others will manage a budget very proficiently right out of the gate. Their position within the museum won't always be an indicator of their aptitude with numbers, by the way. I've seen educators with no financial experience handle a budget with ease and accountants struggle to produce concise reports. This actually makes sense when you think about it. Educators are good at communication and connecting dots, while we analytical types tend to overthink things.

Leaving Some Things to the Imagination

As you build financial literacy and communication within your institution, it's also important to determine who needs to know what, in what format, and when. While I'm an advocate of being open and accessible, I don't recommend transparency just for the sake of transparency. Overwhelming people with every detail about the financial state of the museum won't create greater engagement. If you're involved with managing a budget and comfortable with numbers, you may be eager to share projections and in-depth information. I've probably caused many eyes to glaze over in my day. Yet, a detailed budget will rarely be meaningful to people who are new to budgeting or haven't been involved with the process. Sharing detailed financial information without context can even lead to misconceptions or cause alarm.

Rather, transparency works best when it's targeted and thoughtful. The level of information you provide should be in the service of the expected outcome. Figure out what's important to people and shape the metrics and information about it. Are you trying to demonstrate that revenue is down, and that expenses are up? Or that the institution has spent more in one area in order to accomplish strategic initiatives? Or do you need to share concerns about troubling financial trends? Sharing targeted information can also be strategic. If the museum is performing well in some areas, but has challenges in others, you can show what you want to show. Maybe you want to focus on successes because the museum is headed in the right direction. Or perhaps you need to highlight the challenges in order to encourage fundraising or more prudent financial management.

You may choose to adjust your approach based on external factors or pressures as well. For example, I routinely share budget projections for the year with the senior staff members at our museum. I show them the projected revenue amounts and how our projected expenses compare. I believe it helps promote transparency and helps us put activities in context. This information helps increase their financial literacy because they see how expenses compare to revenue. But in certain years, I hold these projections back or only share a summary view. For example, during the COVID-19 pandemic, our projections were all over the board. While I was updating them frequently, and sharing them with the director, I felt that sharing them more openly would become confusing. We weren't in financial trouble, fortunately, but I wanted to buffer senior staff from the chaotic adjustments that characterized that year. They had their own priorities to worry about, and it was enough to reassure them that we were financially stable. It was also a year that wasn't representative of our regular operation, so sharing detailed projections may have been misleading. Financial literacy doesn't require knowing everything all of the time, it requires knowing the information that is meaningful at the right time.

In some circumstances, it also makes sense to layer the amount of information you're presenting. For example, at a board meeting, you may wish to create a financial summary and then provide supporting detail for members who are interested in seeing more. Board members with an extensive business background, however, may want to go right to the details and grow impatient with glossy summaries. With some boards, you may need to provide both. Before you create a presentation or report, consider your audience. Tailor it to them as well as you can. Give people of different backgrounds and interests different ways into the information. This gives them the tools to work with the numbers in a meaningful way and to develop literacy at their own pace.

Show Me the Money

People learn in different ways and providing information in a variety of formats can create more meaningful engagement. For many staff members and stakeholders, visual representations such as pie charts or graphs can help distill a concept or trend into something more easily understood. The field of data visualization is rapidly developing and is really intriguing for financial reporting. Maybe this book should be called "beyond the pie charts." Pie charts are sometimes exactly what you need, but you also might build a compelling visualization with scatter charts, timelines, or even animations. If you present financial data to others, it's worth thinking through effective and compelling visual models. The best visualizations immediately and powerfully convey the point you're trying to make (not necessarily an easy task). Often this means telling a story with the numbers. We're a visual field, so naturally people who work in museums tend to react positively to visual representations. Literacy does not have to mean reading numbers or text, it might mean recognizing associations or seeing trends. It's primarily about developing understanding, however it's obtained.

Cats in Suits

Humor is another great way to build financial literacy with a minimum of pain. Anyone who has gone through a budget discussion with me knows that there might be a cat in a business suit on one of the slides. Budgeting rarely includes a sense of humor, but I think it can be fun to drop in some things that are unexpected. I know it probably results in some eye rolls, but I make them suffer through it. You have to admit, if you knew there would be a cat in a suit, you'd be watching a little more closely. There's a time and place for humor, of course. I wouldn't present a budget report to our advisory council with that kind of format. But internally, we have a pretty good rapport and sense of trust with each other. So, it's become a bit of a running joke and is all in good fun. I think it can also diffuse the discomfort and boredom that sometimes goes along with budgeting, and helps people see the lighter side. A colleague at the Portland Art Museum, Gareth Nevitt, said that "budgeting is too serious to take seriously." And I couldn't agree more. Here are some additional ideas for bringing humor or lightness into budget discussions:

- Use money-themed treats, such as chocolate coins in gold foil, or cupcakes with dollar signs, to celebrate accomplishments like wrapping up a financial year or sticking to a budget. Treats can also be used to encourage questions and discussion, for example, handing out a gold coin for the person who volunteers to present first.
- Try ridiculous presentation themes or images, such as cats on water skis. They should not relate to budgeting in any way.
- Treat budgeting as a board game and use piles of jellybeans or tokens to represent budget allocations. Eat the jellybeans as the budget is expended.
- When reporting on budget trends, use a theme such as "The Good, The Bad, and The Ugly."
- Give departments slogans as if they were beach volleyball teams, such as "Team Curatorial: We get to handle all of the objects."
- Use money-themed songs or movie clips during presentations, breaks, or when people are filtering into the room.

Rinse and Repeat

As with any new skill or concept, repetition and consistency are key. The first time you set up a budget, the process will probably be a bit cumbersome. It may take you a long time to research and project expenses. You might build in too much of a cushion, or no cushion at all. That's completely okay. The second time you set up a budget, you will be better at it. The annual budget cycle lends itself to improvement and refinement. If your institution uses fiscal year planning and quarterly reviews, you'll see these numbers at least four times throughout the year. Then you'll close one fiscal year cycle and begin again. This might feel like a circle of hell to some people, but it's also predictable. It's a built-in interval for you to continue practicing your skills. If you made a mess of your fiscal year predictions, that's okay, just correct it during the first quarter review. Did you fall asleep during the first quarter review meeting? Completely not okay, but you can do better during the second quarter. That's the elegance of the quarterly review system, it's cyclical and iterative, and there are opportunities for constant improvement and correction.

For this reason, the institutional budget process benefits from consistent formats and timelines. While financial literacy requires some skill with formats and formulas, the most important part of literacy is the planning and projections themselves. Whatever format you settle on for your institution, budget sheets should become like old friends. When a budget manager clicks open their sheet, the format will be similar to the previous quarter and the previous fiscal year. Then the effort can be focused on strategic planning, not on the layout of the spreadsheet. This applies to summary financial reports for the institution as well. If you're not in an institution where there's a required standard, you might be creating reports on your own. Try to identify the best format for your financial report and stick to it year after year. You can spin things off from it, of course, such as presentations for a particular audience, but keep the core report consistent. This not only makes reports easier to compile but also allows the institution to see trends more clearly. Financial people love to create reports, but a folder full of information in different formats adds to confusion and gatekeeping. Consistency lends itself to learning and literacy, particularly for people who are not really that excited to be budgeting in the first place. If you're proficient with financial issues, you can support the financial literacy of others by using consistent and accessible formats for financial reports.

Read About It

Another way to increase financial literacy is to make it a topic of professional development and staff readings. If you're fortunate, your museum staff already reads books and articles together on topics such as interpretation, equity, and accessibility. But has any museum staff in the history of time read an article or book on financial management or budget issues together? Probably not. Unfortunately, despite the substantial impact they have, budgets and resource management just aren't hot topics in the field. Yet, there are numerous articles and books that could be the basis for a staff discussion (hmm, may I suggest this one?). As with most topics, some staff members will find them an easy read and have a lot to add to the discussion. Others may struggle or find some of the information inaccessible. But being uncomfortable or out of your depth isn't a reason to avoid a topic, it's often a good reason to tackle it. Trust me, most museum administrators have sat through dozens of presentations on curatorial and education topics, even though they don't have any expertise in these areas. They may not understand everything, but they pay attention because these things matter. But so does financial literacy. So, get ready for some payback.

The very process of assigning a book or article, and discussing it, builds financial literacy but it also shows a commitment to changing culture. It demonstrates what leadership values. It can build vocabulary and concepts in an open way. It can also be a good way to frame discussions about the museum's own financial situation. For example, in one institution, we were facing a downturn in the economy. A staff member had read an article about a peer museum having financial issues and questioned if we would be vulnerable to the same problems. This turned into an excellent opportunity to discuss the museum's funding model (which was quite different from the peer institution) and alleviate some concerns. It still would have been a valuable discussion if the museum had been facing the same issues. We could have discussed how the funds are managed and what safeguards we had in place. Or it might have been a chance to discuss some real concerns. Reading the article gave the staff member the vocabulary to ask insightful questions, and the confidence to raise the issue in the first place. Once we start normalizing financial discussions, staff members outside of administration will feel more empowered to ask questions and provide input.

Budget Minute

Along with staff discussions prompted by books and articles, budgeting and financial issues should have a standing place on staff meeting agendas. One technique that can work well for dense topics such as budgeting is to schedule a "budget minute." Instead of trying to present a budget projection for the entire fiscal year, the budget minute tackles a small concept in a short amount of time (it could be longer than a minute). For example, you might explain how endowments are structured and used, or highlight one of the restricted funds managed by the museum. Keeping the discussions quick and focused helps hold attention and gives people only one thing to absorb. And you might be surprised at the cumulative knowledge it can build over time. If a "budget minute" is incorporated into a standing meeting only once a month, staff members will build knowledge on twelve different concepts within a year. We also use this technique for other (potentially) yawn-inducing topics, such as emergency management, and find that it's effective and painless. It can even provoke interesting discussions and be sort of fun. It keeps things top-of-mind but doesn't overwhelm people with too much information at once.

You can also use this technique to build your own financial literacy. If you're interested in learning more about retirement planning, for example (and who isn't??), you can challenge yourself to spend five to fifteen minutes a week reading about the topic. That's enough time to finish a short article over lunch on a Friday. It may not seem like a lot, but it adds up and can result in some impressive cumulative knowledge. When it comes to building financial literacy, small commitments can be more effective than sweeping changes.

Budget Buddy

Like many goals, it can be helpful to find a friend or colleague who is also interested in increasing their financial literacy. You can do readings together, have discussions over lunch, or help each other with questions. It can be like a mini book club. If it's a work colleague, you can also support each other in meetings by mirroring back and acknowledging each other's contributions. It can also help to have someone else to review your budget planning and catch issues, or gently challenge your assumptions. It can be motivating to learn with someone else and encourage each other along the way. This also works well for personal financial goals, such as increasing retirement savings or supporting each other in asking for a pay increase.

Getting Personal

Another great way to increase your knowledge of how budgets function is to build the skills with your own personal or household budget. Budgets are budgets, whether they're for a household of one person or for a large corporation. So, while some things will be different, the skills are transferrable (in both directions). If you're committed to learning these skills for your career, you might as well develop them, in parallel, in your personal life. This can also help you recognize the impact of salary increases (or lack of increases), and how other financial issues in your career filter over to your personal financial situation. As you progress with financial literacy, you'll probably find that you develop a natural curiosity and proficiency with money management in general.

If you're not careful, you might also become more interested in the financial aspects of other benefits your employer (hopefully) offers, such as retirement plans or sick leave credits. Those are all forms of compensation as well, and, especially in public museums, benefits can be complex—you may easily overlook some of the features. Here are a few suggestions for increasing your financial literacy with personal finance:

- If you don't already have one, set up a household budget using free online software. There are many user-friendly choices out there that can link right to your accounts. If you haven't had a budget before, you might be surprised at where you're spending your money versus where you think you're spending it. This will also give you some practice in projecting budgets and understanding why things sometimes go off track.
- If you have a retirement account, figure out what it's invested in and read over the prospectus. You might not understand everything you read, but see if you can discover something new about how your money is invested. Chances are you don't even know which companies you're currently supporting. Are they in line with your values?
- If you're fortunate enough to have benefits at work, pick one of the programs to learn more about. Read the brochure that you probably skimmed over or ignored when you were hired. For example, read about the life insurance program so that you understand exactly how much it costs and what benefits you, or your beneficiaries, would receive. If there are options to choose from, is it optimized and set up the way you would like? If not, then follow through and fill out the form to make the change. Right away. Don't put it aside or you might forget.
- If you already have a retirement fund at work and are taking full advantage of any employer match, consider setting one up outside of work, such as a Roth IRA. The process of investigating and setting up an account can teach you a lot, even if your contribution is small. Most large brokers offer them

for free or at low cost. It can be hard to get started, but you'll thank yourself in future years.

A Word About Negotiation

As you build financial literacy, you'll become more empowered to negotiate for yourself and others. As someone who often sits on the other side of the table, I wanted to share a few thoughts about what makes an effective case in salary negotiation. First, always lead with your strengths. What can you bring or offer the museum? Do you have particular skills that are in short supply? Can you say that the interview went well and that they would really like to hire you? Or, if you're already in a position, do you bring particular values that would be hard to replace? Negotiate from this position of strength. Second, we talk a lot about living wage and cost of living. These are important considerations, but be careful about how you frame them. A hiring manager won't be swayed by the argument that your bills are high or that you live in an expensive area of the city. They won't pay you more because you have two kids instead of one. These are important issues to you personally, of course, and might be factored into the salary you're requesting. But they're not effective in a negotiation. While most museums are nonprofit, they're also businesses and are negotiating with their budget and operation in mind. They will, however, be conscious of factors like retention, or the need to make a great hire. They'll also be thinking about market data and salary equity (with comparable positions, not with positions in different fields). It doesn't matter if your personal rent is high, but it does matter if the museum ten blocks away is paying more. If the museum doesn't compensate people appropriately, they'll eventually have recruiting and retention challenges. Finally, don't ever hesitate to negotiate. Sometimes there really is no room on the salary they're offering. But this is rare. If they really want to hire you, they can probably find a little more. And it almost never hurts to ask. In fact, it shows them that you know your own value (based on your strengths and knowledge of your market data, not your rent). Negotiating your salary every time you move positions can make a tremendous difference in your overall lifetime earnings and in your personal financial security. It also advances the salaries of the overall field. If you're not comfortable negotiating on your own behalf, then think of it as negotiating for future generations of museum workers. If you're concerned about salary equity and compensation in the museum field, then you have a responsibility to negotiate. You can do it with a smile but should still negotiate.

Building financial literacy is a process. It takes time, but it can be rewarding and even enjoyable. It's essential for museum leadership positions and will provide the tools for greater engagement in the strategic direction of your museum, no matter what your current position. Confidence and ease with budgeting can change the course of your career and sometimes even your life. It will give you the skills and knowledge to effectively negotiate for yourself and others. Invest in yourself by identifying and committing to small steps to increase financial literacy and empowerment.

Three Ways to Expand Your Financial Knowledge:

1. Find a financial blog or website that seems accessible and subscribe to it or read the top five articles.
2. Look up the living wage in your city (if there is one), as well as the median salary for your position in the museum field. You can find this through salary surveys published by the large professional organizations in the field.
3. Think about something you'd like to negotiate for and take time to build a compelling argument about how it would benefit the *other* party.

9

✣

Understanding and Projecting Revenue

M anaging a budget doesn't necessarily require a knowledge of where the revenue originates, but understanding museum funding models can help you expand your knowledge of how budgets function. Most museums operate on a mix of revenue and funding types, which have different strengths and weaknesses. Revenue and funding types vary considerably depending on the type and size of museum. For some museums, their funding model includes earned revenue, government funding, and contributed revenue. For others, it might comprise earned revenue, grant revenue, and private funding. A museum might have only one or two sources of funding, or it might have a dozen. The following information about revenue is common to museums throughout the world, but every institution has its own mix of these categories.

The Three-Legged Stool: Building Stability

Whatever the mix, there's an advantage to diversifying funding, or developing a broad mix of funding and revenue from different sources. Using a variety of funding and revenue types protects the institution better against downturns or losses in one of the areas. A very large economic downturn or event may affect all revenue and funding categories at the same time, but this would be relatively unusual. So, diversity provides stability. A variety of funding also promotes growth and creates opportunity.

To demonstrate how funding types react differently to downturns, we can consider an extreme example. During the COVID-19 pandemic, for example, nearly all museums experienced financial uncertainty. But the timing and severity varied according to their funding model. Museums that relied heavily on earned revenue, such as admission, rentals, and store revenue, took an immediate hit. The revenue dried up overnight when the doors closed. These museums needed to be open to generate most of their earned revenue, and closures (whether mandated or voluntary) had a severe and rapid impact. For example, the Milwaukee Art

Museum reported losing $10,000 a day during its closure. This was largely due to the loss of revenue from admissions, store sales, and facility rentals. Museums relying more heavily on contributed income, such as gifts, were more insulated initially. They also experienced difficulties, however. Donors were also enduring financial hardship and might have reduced their giving, or diverted their giving to more urgent causes such as healthcare. Museums using endowment income were somewhat insulated. Although there was a significant market downturn early in the pandemic, endowments tend to have safeguards that smooth the losses over time. Museums receiving government funding were the most insulated of all, at least initially, because they tend to have more stable funding. Yet, they experienced impacts on a longer time horizon as budgets were cut in order to control spending. All of these situations presented challenges. An institution with a varied mix of funding would experience less severe and immediate reductions. Diverse funding creates a staggered timeline of reductions, which allow museums to more strategically manage the downturn.

Developing a varied mix of funding sources provides stability for the organization. Each type of funding contributes its own strengths as well as its own weaknesses. When used together, they can shore up one another and create a solid foundation. A good analogy for the stability of multiple funding sources is a wooden stool. A stool will not stand very long, or maybe at all, with one leg. If you have one type of revenue, you're relying too heavily on that single leg. It's asking a lot of only one leg, and the stool won't be well-balanced or stable. Even if that leg is strong, the stool will fall if it's pulled out from under you. You'll do better if you can have two legs, or two sources of revenue, although it will still be a bit wobbly. And if you can add a third leg, you'll find that it's fairly stable. The ideal funding model is a balanced mix, or a three-legged stool. Some museums will have a four- or five-legged stool, and that's fine too, as long as it's not unwieldy to manage. If you have only one or two sources, however, then you're at more risk. Three-legged stools may not have perfectly even legs. For example, a government-funded museum probably receives a large share of support from government funding and may not have a robust earned revenue program. But moving *closer* to a model of three balanced funding sources will provide more flexibility and strength. The origins of these funding sources are all very different, so only significant events would cause a downturn in all three. The timing of impacts is also different, which offers additional protection. Earned revenue, for example, tends to react very quickly to changes. Contributed revenue can decline, but it tends to take a while. And government funding typically reacts most slowly of all, because it often operates on a biennial or extended budget cycle. So, by incorporating all three sources you create additional buffers and smooth out the downturns.

Variable versus Stable

Another way to diversify your funding streams is to use a mix of both variable and stable revenue or funding. These terms loosely capture how likely the funding is to change from year to year, and over longer time periods. Determining the degree of variability or stability of your funding streams will help you create more accurate budget projections, and also help you assess the level of risk in your funding model. These categories can encompass a variety of programs and initiatives, so they don't always fit into neat categories. Generally, funding can be categorized from most stable to least stable as follows:

- government funding
- endowment income
- gifts and membership
- earned revenue
- grants

The stability of a funding stream is often in inverse proportion to its growth potential. For example, government museums enjoy a consistent level of support, but they struggle to obtain funding increases or new positions. Municipal museums may survive on less stable revenue but, when they're doing well, they can often support larger staffs and operating budgets. These categories might not hold true at every institution or every program but, in general, the more variable the revenue, the more potential it has for growth. The more stable the revenue or funding, the more likely it is to plateau. Due to all of these different factors, timelines, and risks, the ideal model is to balance variable revenue with more stable funding types in order to reduce overall volatility. These factors can also help your institution determine where it should shore up its funding model. If you have very stable revenue, you might want to develop more entrepreneurial programs so you become more dynamic and self-sufficient. And if you already have a lot of earned revenue, then you will want to pursue a more stable form of support that will help you endure more difficult or unpredictable economic times.

Leaning on Stability

Government Funding

The best example of a stable funding source is government funding, such as state or federal support. This is sometimes called a government "allocation," because it's been allocated in a budget bill or document. Government funding typically, but not always, is stable over time. You can generally count on it without too many concerns. If you rely more heavily on stable funding, then you're in a fortunate position and your institution is less likely to face financial hardships. In truth, however, almost any source of funding is variable over the long term. A common pitfall in government museums is to assume that stable funding will never change. This can lead to complacency. During good financial times, you might not be capitalizing on other funding opportunities or you might not take budgeting seriously enough. You may not be focused enough about using your resources to achieve your strategic priorities. Museum staff members might not be participating in advocacy or actively engaging with decision makers. You may not be adequately demonstrating your value to the public you serve. During bad financial times, however, the results can be disastrous. Government museums tend to rely heavily on government support and a budget cut to that funding can decimate the institution. If your government museum hasn't developed additional revenue streams, your very existence may hinge on budget decisions outside of your control. If that concerns you, it should.

One advantage to stable government funding, however, is that you can stay informed about budget decisions and often have advance notice of cuts. These dangers can lurk under the surface if you're not monitoring the budget process at a higher level or if your director or board isn't privy to this kind of information. For this reason, it's helpful to develop an awareness of where that stable funding originates. For example, for a state or university museum, government funding is likely coming down through the state budget process. If you have responsibility for institutional budgeting, you may find it valuable to sit in on budget discussions at your parent agency. Public agencies are required to adhere to a large degree of transparency and advance notice regarding the budgeting process and related meetings. Use this to your advantage and keep tabs on what's happening. Even if you sit in on a meeting and understand half of it, you're increasing your knowledge and ability to navigate the process. You'll get to recognize the people making decisions and understand the positions they take on budget allocations. You may even find opportunities to advocate for your museum. Advocacy doesn't have to be complex or intimidating. It might mean introducing yourself on a break, or writing a letter to thank a legislator for their support during the budget process. At our organization, for example, we include elected officials on our mailing list so they receive notice of our new exhibitions and public events. These small things can remind decision makers of the value of your institution.

Another advantage to engaging with the budgeting process is knowing how to time and make strategic requests for more resources. For government museums, requests for new funding also often have to be made far in advance in order to align with the state or university budgeting processes. If you know what's happening with the budget of your parent agency, it will help you determine if the time is right to request more funding or new positions. You can also determine when the time isn't right, and demonstrate an awareness and consideration of the challenges being experienced by your parent agency.

As a trade-off to the stability of government funding, the challenge for government-funded museums is that growth is limited. Government budgets are cyclical and frequently stretched, so securing new positions or funding is often a challenge. While decision makers may value the museum, they are often faced with limited resources and difficult decisions regarding priorities. Particularly if the museum is buried under other parent agencies, it may be difficult to move the needle on the allocated budget. Due to their reliance on stable funding, government museums may also not have well-developed earned revenue programs or the staffing to support them. This is changing as government museums recognize the need to develop more self-sufficiency and become more proactive about earned revenue, development, and grant funding.

Stable funding often comes with other advantages, as well. While the direct operating budget provided to a museum may plateau, government agencies tend to provide extensive support in the form of maintenance, lease costs, security, legal counsel, human resources, and IT support, among others. While we often don't adequately measure the value of all these services and benefits, they are part of the budget as well. As a result, with rare exceptions, government museums tend to be stable and financially sustainable. The trade-off is limited growth, less agility, and a high level of bureaucracy.

Endowment Income

Another form of relatively stable revenue is endowment income. Many museums have endowments, or taken together sometimes referred to as "an" endowment. Endowments are large sums of money, typically at least $50,000 that are invested by, or on behalf of, the museum. The "principal" or the endowment itself is the large sum of money that is invested (i.e., the $50,000). The "income" is the interest generated by that investment. The interest income may be considered "earned" revenue, which acknowledges that interest is being "earned" on the investment. Other museums may loosely categorize endowment income as contributed income because the original principal was contributed. Most endowments are permanent, which means the museum can only use a certain level of endowment income, not the endowment principal itself. Endowments are a particularly powerful form of support because they are the "gifts that keep on giving." If managed well, an endowment should help support the museum in perpetuity.

Endowments grow in value and generate income because they're invested, usually in a mix of stocks, bonds, and other securities. If you ever watch the performance of the S&P 500, you'll have a sense of how the market is doing. The S&P 500 is an index and an indicator of the stock market, but it doesn't necessarily represent the particular investments of any given endowment. But because endowments are invested, their value will typically fluctuate substantially over time. Despite this volatility, careful management actually makes endowment income a stable form of support.

One of the management strategies for endowments is determining the appropriate level of endowment income to use each year. If you spend too much, you will eventually reduce the principal. If you take too little, the principal will grow but you won't be fully leveraging the endowment for support of the museum. Some endowments may generate income based on their actual investment performance. So, for example, if an endowment grows by 10 percent annually, the museum will access the 10 percent. This can be problematic if the investment is down, however. If endowment income was assessed based on actual performance, there might be years where growth is nonexistent or even negative. For this reason, most endowments are managed using a spending policy. The policy establishes a percentage for the income, such as 6 percent of the endowment value, regardless of what the investment is actually earning. So, for example, a $1,000,000 endowment would generate $60,000 in annual income. This amount is typically distributed by quarter, so $15,000 each quarter. By keeping this percentage fairly conservative, an endowment can endure ups and downs in the market while still retaining its value. This is, by the way, also a common approach to managing retirement funds.

Along with determining the appropriate percentage of income to spend each year, investment managers have to decide how to determine the base amount they are calculating it on. For example, a $1,000,000 investment might actually be worth $890,000 or $1,100,000 at any given point in time. To cushion against this fluctuation, the base amount may be "smoothed" to avoid volatility and overspending. For example, our foundation uses a sixteen-quarter system to determine the base amount. They calculate the value of the endowment averaged over the past sixteen quarters, and then generate 6 percent annually on that base amount. Using these two methods, our endowment income is remarkably stable and predictable. It would take a long and severe downturn to impact the annual amount of endowment income available to the museum. If this is too technical, please don't be concerned about it. It's enough to know that endowments are investments that require careful management, but they're a strong and stable source of support.

Most endowments are considered "permanent" because, in theory and with careful management, they should go on in perpetuity. Using these management techniques, the principal, or large lump sum, should remain in place over time. Endowments can also be designated as "temporary," which means the principal is left intact temporarily. Sometimes they're temporary for a particular number of years, or until certain conditions are met. For example, a donor might provide a large lump sum that is treated as an endowment until her art collection is donated by her future estate. The principal will remain unspent until that event occurs. At that point, the museum may continue using only endowment income, or it may start to draw down the principal itself. Temporary endowments may also be established in order to give the museum director or board more flexibility. For example, in difficult economic times the museum may need to access some of the endowment principal. Or the principal might be accessed for a particular strategic use, such as the acquisition of a particular type of artwork or support of a major exhibition. Every endowment will be slightly different, so it's a good idea to carefully review terms and conditions and to understand how they're managed.

Endowments are an ideal funding source due to their longevity. If managed well, they are a fairly stable and predictable form of revenue as well. There are a few downsides to endowments, however. If an endowment is permanent, the principal can't be accessed. So, the large lump sum is essentially locked up. And endowments take a while to begin generating income. So, if you have a big fundraising push to create an endowment, you won't see the benefits for a while. And, while building an endowment is a worthwhile initiative, it may temporarily divert gifts that would have been given in cash. This can be a strategic decision, but the museum may need to weather a short-term downturn for a long-term gain. An endowment also needs to be fairly large to generate a substantial amount of income each year. These factors make it hard to build endowments, but they're very valuable once they're in place.

Balancing Volatility

Unlike stable funding, such as government allocations and endowment income, variable revenue tends to fluctuate from year to year. Variable revenue is harder to predict, which makes it harder to budget against. Examples in this category are earned revenue, gifts, and grants. This type of funding or revenue is responsive to changes in the world around us. An example is earned revenue from the museum store or from admission. If the museum closes unexpectedly, this revenue can dry up almost overnight. Gifts might be more predictable, but philanthropic giving also reacts to the economy. Donors might choose to give to more urgent causes or have challenges in their own financial situation. This is especially true if a museum relies on a small number of donors for large gifts. If one of those donors goes elsewhere, it can have a large impact on your funding. If you rely more heavily on variable revenue, and many museums do, then you're in a more precarious situation and you'll want to spend more time analyzing your projected revenue and creating contingency plans.

Gift Funds and Membership

Gift funds include direct cash gifts given to the museum. These typically come in through an annual appeal, or as small cash gifts throughout the year, such as those collected in donation boxes. In this context, "cash" means gifts that can be spent directly. Generally, gifts will be spent within three years or less unless they are designated for a specific purpose. Some donors have a consistent giving pattern; they may give a particular amount on an annual basis. Others will give on a less predictable interval, such as to a particular development initiative or to support a favorite program. Gifts can also vary a lot in amount and level of donor engagement. Some of the museum's strongest and most active supporters may give small amounts, while less involved stakeholders such as large corporations may give large amounts. Due to all of the variables, gift revenue can be challenging to project for budgeting purposes. Even when using historical information, gift revenue may not be completely predictable from year to year.

Many museums also have a membership program. Membership revenue is often considered a gift, although some museums consider it earned revenue. Some museums even divide it up due to tax reporting requirements. For example, if you receive a benefit from membership the value of that item may be earned revenue (an exchange with the museum), while the remainder may be gift revenue (freely contributed, with nothing of value received in return). The particular division between these two revenue categories, if any, will depend on the incentives associated with your membership program.

Membership is another area where it's incredibly important to understand the goals and expected outcome. Is the membership program primarily for revenue? Or is it for creating a connection with visitors? The Dallas Museum of Art made an interesting and newsworthy change when it made its membership program free. This reflected an acknowledgment that the primary purpose of the program was audience engagement. It also prioritized accessibility, removing the potential barrier of cost. Some museums may rely on membership revenue and this type of approach may not be possible. At the Chazen Museum, we made a change to our membership program in recent years. Instead of the membership dues and tiers that we previously used, we started treating nearly all donors as members. There were still "perks" based on giving levels, but it made our entire donor base into our membership base. This also streamlined management of the membership program, which became more focused on donor stewardship rather than administration. We still plan special member events and offer benefits, but this move acknowledged that our membership program was primarily philanthropic.

The museum offers free admission, so this shift made sense because our members weren't joining to obtain reduced admission or other transactional perks. It's worthwhile to consider the objectives of your membership program and align your approach accordingly.

Earned Revenue

Earned revenue is primarily brought in by the business activities of a museum. Examples of earned revenue include admission fees, retail store revenue, facility rentals, and photography fees. Some museums may also include endowment income and membership (or some portion of it) in earned revenue. Here, however, earned revenue mostly refers to revenue earned through specific activities such as the operation of the museum store or paid admission. It would be rare for a museum to operate solely on earned revenue. Examples of museum who might operate this way are corporate museums. There are even some museums operating on a for-profit basis. On the other end of the spectrum are government museums, who tend to lag behind in earned revenue. Most museums fall in the middle and have at least some earned revenues in their funding models. Relying heavily on earned revenue (outside of endowment income) carries risk due to its volatility.

Earned revenue is generally variable, meaning it varies from year to year. If bad weather and construction keeps visitors away from the museum, earned revenue may also decrease for the year. If a large exhibit drives visitation, however, it might increase for the year. This sometimes makes earned revenue difficult to project and the effects of a downturn can be felt very quickly. This is also a category of revenue that may not have a secondary source of funding to fall back on. Earned revenue may go directly to staff member salaries, program supplies, or items to be sold in the gift store. This is why these areas see hits fairly quickly if the museum closes unexpectedly. This area of the museum tends to operate like a business and experiences the same economic cycles. While earned revenue programs often have a connection to the mission, they are expected to be largely self-sufficient. Even the most generous donors don't want to bail out a failing museum store or shore up a rental program.

Earned revenue also has a lot of potential, however, because it's a funding category that the museum can proactively change. It's one of the most dynamic categories of funding and an area of potential growth. Along with its volatility, earned revenue offers the possibility of entrepreneurial growth. There is sometimes a tension between the mission of a museum and its supporting earned revenue programs. They can easily drift afield of the museum's mission. If a museum desperately needs income, it might find itself supporting activities that ignore, or even contradict, its strategic priorities. Planning a new earned revenue program requires a careful evaluation of the costs and objectives, and how the profit can be balanced with the mission.

You can start a lively debate at your museum by asking if the museum store exists for the sake of profit or in support of the mission. It ideally should do both, but some museum stores barely break even or operate at a loss. A store like that wouldn't last long in the for-profit world, but the museum may subsidize the operation of the retail space as a visitor amenity and a source of promotion. For example, the store might sell branded merchandise, catalogues with contributions by the museum's curators, or products connected to current exhibitions. Or the museum may have a large, profitable store that sells generic merchandise not clearly connected to the mission of the institution. Or a museum may have a lucrative business in space rentals, but it might require that the areas are closed to public access during certain times. There are trade-offs with all of these initiatives. If you have any involvement with an earned revenue program, it's worthwhile to review your financial and institutional goals. There's nothing inherently wrong with subsidizing a store or prioritizing profit over public access within certain parameters, but stakeholders need to be clear on the intent and implications of those decisions. Unlike many for-profit businesses, financial measures aren't enough to fully evaluate decisions about earned revenue. If the earned revenue program isn't furthering the mission in some way, then it might be time to reevaluate.

Grants

Many museums receive a small percentage of their funding from grants. Grants can come from a variety of funders, such as corporate or family foundations and government agencies. Grants generally have clear guidelines for use of funds and have established reporting requirements. Funding agencies may require a contract or written agreement regarding use of the funds. Many (but not all) grants are provided for specific projects, with a clear timeline, outcome, and required evaluation. These formal applications and reporting requirements help distinguish a grant from a gift.

Grants are generally variable, meaning they can't be counted on year to year. The museum may apply and not necessarily know if funding will be received. In other cases, grants are largely recurring and are provided on a regular annual basis. Grants can be a great source of support for discretionary initiatives, such as conservation or new outreach programs. They're less appealing for general ongoing support, because they tend to have extensive reporting requirements and laborious application procedures. This is understandable, because funding agencies want to be sure that funding is distributed equitably and that it's used effectively and responsibly. They also want some credit and publicity for their support. Grants can serve as a nice supplement to the museum's funding and revenue, but it's worth assessing the time and effort against the funding that will be potentially received. In some cases, for example, a museum may decide only to pursue larger grants that will have a significant impact on their program. Or they may determine that grants are best used for support of specific initiatives such as conservation. Sometimes grants serve as a bridge to other community organizations, creating opportunities for partnerships and mutual support.

Whatever method a museum uses for grant development, getting out ahead of the planning will help to create a strategic approach. Grants typically require applications far in advance. Some foundations also require a "letter of inquiry" before even allowing an application. Particularly if you don't have a dedicated staff member working on grants, you will want to carefully consider which grants are the best fit for your institution. You might find value in creating a grant spreadsheet that identifies interesting funding opportunities, application deadlines, and other details. You can review it annually, or quarterly, and decide which ones to pursue. Identifying grant opportunities near the start of each fiscal year, for example, can help you better plan and project grant revenue.

Techniques for Managing Variable Revenue

Due to its unpredictability, it can be challenging to accurately predict variable revenue. There are numerous factors that can affect the amount of variable revenue received in a year. The amount of revenue might be impacted by the exhibition schedule, level of marketing, competing events in your area, connection to social issues, performance of the stock market, unemployment, construction, and even the weather in some parts of the country. Creating accurate projections is difficult, but getting a handle on this category is necessary for financial sustainability. If your museum doesn't have a reserve, you may be spending revenue in the same year or even quarter you receive it. For example, as you plan for the upcoming fiscal year, you might project that you will bring in $100,000 in gifts. This is only a projection, so there is a chance the estimate will be too low or too high. In fact, the odds that you will bring in exactly $100,000 are pretty slim. If you've planned your spending around the $100,000 projection, you may find yourself with a problem on your hands if gifts are lower than expected. If revenue falls short of projections, but spending continues as planned, you may create a deficit or have to pull back on expenses.

Trying to assess and analyze all of the factors can be overwhelming, but there are a few techniques for projecting and managing variable revenue. One method you can use for projecting variable revenue is to get one year ahead and budget based on the amount you received in the *previous* year. So, last year you might have brought in $80,000 in gifts. You will limit your spending to $80,000 this year, even though you think you will probably bring in $100,000 in gifts. There are several caveats to this approach. One is that you first need a reserve (savings) of approximately one year. If you don't have a reserve, then you won't have a cushion for the lean years. So, for example, if you brought in $100,000 last year but only $80,000 this year, you can't plan to spend $100,000 unless you have a reserve to draw on. Hopefully, your variable revenue will increase every year, but there may be times it decreases due to factors outside of your control. If you have a small reserve, then it gives you a cushion for your spending to ebb and flow. Having a reserve of one year is unrealistic for some institutions. In that case, you can use a modified approach of budgeting revenue by quarter or by half year.

Another caveat is that the technique of budgeting based on last year's revenue creates delayed gratification, as well as delayed pain. So, while the economy is doing well, and you have a banner year for gifts, your institution has to be prepared to live on less than you're actually bringing in. You have to bank the excess as a reserve for a future lean year. On the other hand, unexpected downturns in giving won't really affect you, because they won't have an impact until the following fiscal year, which gives you plenty of time to plan. This approach requires some discipline and advance planning but is an effective way of creating a rolling reserve to see you through leaner times.

You can also use a similar technique and budget against a running average of several years. So, for example, if in the past three years you brought in $80,000, $50,000, and then $100,000 in gifts, you would budget about $77,000 a year (the average of the three years). You can see that in the years when you brought in more that you'll be "banking" the surplus. In the year when you brought in less, you'll have enough to budget $77,000 due to your reserve. Every year you'll then also update the running average, so the amount keeps pace with the overall trend. So, if gifts start to trend up you can spend a little more. But if they trend down, your average will also start to adjust. This method will take a little time to implement and also works best if you do have a small reserve to cushion against a series of low years.

Another method for managing variable revenue is to assess it carefully during quarterly budget reviews. If revenue is falling short of projections, then you'll have time to recognize this and make adjustments before you end the year with a variance or deficit. This is a particularly good method to use if you have some control over expenses and can tighten things up if revenue falls short. In some cases, you may also be able to structure larger or more discretionary expenses for the second half of the fiscal year. Or you may be required to save up, or secure, funding for these initiatives before they even begin.

Another approach for variable revenue management is to pair it with the most discretionary and flexible activities. If you have standing obligations, such as an exhibition contract payment or building lease, pair those with your most stable funding. That way, you'll be able to cover your basic obligations. Then you can pair more variable revenue with activities that can be pulled back if necessary. For example, you might use government funding to pay your lease and contributed gifts to support education. If, during a quarterly budget review, you recognize that giving is lower than expected for the year, you can decide to reduce the size or number of exhibition openings for the remainder of the year. Or maybe you can seek out additional support for those programs. No one likes to change plans unexpectedly, but it's far better to forgo food at an exhibition opening rather than miss a lease payment. Not every funding source is flexible about what it can support, but for those that are, you can be strategic about what type of revenue is supporting what type of expense.

Use Your Discretion: Managing Restrictions

Many types of revenue and funding can also be sorted into two categories: restricted and unrestricted. Restricted gifts, for example, are given by the donor for a specific purpose. Unrestricted or discretionary gifts can be used for any purpose. The difference between restricted and unrestricted is not always clearly delineated. For example, if a donor gives a gift to be used by the education department, it is restricted. Yet it supports day-to-day activities of the education department and can be used how they see fit, as long as it's available only to that section. It must be tracked and used as intended, but there may not be a particular need to make a specific plan to use it. It will support the education department's normal operation. If, on the other hand, a donor gives a gift to support a new named internship program within the education program, then that gift is more highly restricted. It requires the establishment of a new program and more precise accountability. The museum may need to make specific plans to start the new internship program and may need to check with the donor on the parameters of how students are selected. In all cases, a gift must be used for the donor's intended purpose, but the definition of "restricted" funds may vary by institution. If you separate out restricted funds on budgets or financial reports, and most museums do, then you have to be clear and consistent about what "restricted" actually means in your institution.

It's helpful to understand the level of restriction for gifts, endowments, and grants because, otherwise, you may acquire a distorted or incomplete picture of the museum's financial position. For example, stakeholders outside of the museum may be concerned that staffing levels are too low or that layoffs have occurred despite the museum having a large endowment. They may see a surplus carried over year to year and feel it should be used to avoid layoffs or increase staffing. There may be a surplus, but it may be partially, or wholly, restricted. The positions that were laid off may be funded by a very specific funding source, such as earned revenue. Or they may observe that a director's salary is substantially more than that of a junior staff member. While salary equity is an important issue, the funding structure might drive some of those decisions. For example, the director position may be endowed or may use funds restricted for salary support of that position. Those funds may not be available to increase other salaries, even if the director's salary was decreased. Knowing that a museum has a large endowment or an annual surplus is simply not enough information to determine whether they're using funds appropriately. Try to avoid coming to conclusions until you understand the entire funding picture. The management of restrictions is complex and has to be carefully considered when making operating and staffing decisions.

All museums would prefer unrestricted funds because they provide maximum flexibility, but that's not how gifts, endowments, and grants are often received. When receiving gifts, there's often a tension between the donor's wishes and the institution's needs. Discretionary gifts are ideal for museums because they leave the funding available for the highest need of the institution. This also allows significant flexibility over time as priorities and plans change. Donors, however, may have very specific funding ideas due to their own personal or professional interests. Part of development is negotiating these needs to reach a gift agreement that satisfies both the museum and the donor. Sometimes, reaching these agreements is just a matter of communication and mutual education. For example, a donor may want their funding to be used for "conservation." To a museum professional, that's a very specific term. It generally only means conservation treatments, stabilization, and *perhaps* related preservation supplies such as storage boxes. Conservation is important, but it doesn't necessarily support the highest priorities for collections care within a museum. The museum may not have any pressing conservation needs or may still need to establish a clear long-range plan before the funds can effectively be used. The donor, however, may be just as happy with "collections care and conservation." As you can see, this slight modification opens up a much wider variety of activities and needs. For example, now it might be able to support fine art shipping, archival boxes, UV light filters, and environmental monitoring tools, *as well as* conservation treatments when necessary. This designation still meets the donor's wishes but gives the museum more flexibility in how the funds are used. It can even lead to a valuable conversation about how the museum cares for the collection. Sometimes it's about understanding the desire beneath the phrasing in order to translate the donor's intentions into a mutually beneficial agreement. If you don't work in development but access gift or endowment funds, it would be very worthwhile to have a conversation with your development officer to understand current restrictions on funds and how these terms are negotiated. If you are a development officer, specialists on staff can help add more nuance to museum terminology and clarify their department's greatest needs. Navigating institutional needs and donor wishes isn't always easy, but broadening restrictions can help museums better leverage the generosity of their supporters.

Pulling It Together

Most museums operate on a complex mix of funding to include government support, endowment income, gifts, earned revenue, and grants. Moving toward a diversified and resilient mix of funds can help museums weather difficult financial times, as well as grow their self-sufficiency and strength. Assessing the qualities of your current funding model can help you understand the risks and likely challenges your institution will face. It can also help you determine where you should put your focus to develop new funding sources. When it comes to budget management at the section or project level, most of the planning will be done on the expense side. Yet understanding revenue is the key to a more nuanced and strategic approach to budget management.

Three Ways to Expand Your Financial Knowledge:

1. Locate a recent financial or annual report for your museum. Try to determine the largest categories of funding and revenue.
2. If you can compare year to year on the financial report, do the amounts change substantially in any of the categories?
3. Using the financial report, try to determine if your museum has mostly stable or mostly variable funding. If you were in charge of developing your museum's funding model, where might you put the emphasis?

IV

CREATING SUSTAINABILITY

10

✛

Analyzing the Data

Once you have a working budget and have tracked expenses for a while, you have a powerful tool that can provide insights into your organization's operation and priorities. In budgeting, we do tend to focus on the numbers. Yet, underlying all of those numbers are some realities about where you're putting your funding, how programs and sections relate to one another, and how the institution has changed over time. You can pull the numbers apart in nearly infinite ways to gain a better understanding of your institution and how it compares to peer institutions. While a strategic plan represents what an organization aspires to be, a budget represents what it actually is. Your budget offers a tangible way to monitor success on your strategic initiatives and directions. There are a number of useful measures that can quickly be calculated from budgets and financial reports. As you become more familiar with your institutional budget, you can create custom metrics to provide insight into your organization's highest-priority initiatives.

Compensation versus Non-compensation

Comparing compensation to non-compensation can help you gain perspective on your staffing levels and their relationship to programmatic spending. These figures should be relatively easy to find when looking at a financial or annual report. To create a ratio of compensation to non-compensation, you will add up the total spending in each category. For this metric, I recommend using figures from the operating budget (don't include capital expenses, special projects, or art acquisition expenses, for example). First, add up all of the compensation-related expenses. This will include categories such as salary and fringe benefits. Then add up everything else, or just subtract salary from the operating budget total. As you assess salary versus non-salary expenses, there might be a few categories that aren't completely clear. For example, professional development and administrative support costs are closely related to staffing. Yet, for this exercise, they would be considered non-compensation. There may be other forms of financial compensation aside from salary. For example, bonuses. Those would be in the compensation total because they are paid directly to employees. If your museum is under a parent agency, you may also need to calculate fringe benefits that are not directly paid by the museum.

Depending on how your financial report is structured, it might take some time to compile these figures. All of this analysis, however, can offer additional insight into how the organization is funded and how expenses are paid. For the compensation/non-compensation ratio, it's not that important to be precise or get too deep in the weeds about calculations. These figures tend to be large, so small adjustments won't make that much of a difference. If you intend to monitor these numbers over time, you'll just want to be consistent with how you calculate them.

Once you have these figures, you can create a ratio with the compensation total and the non-compensation total. For example, if your institution spends $1,000,000 total on salary and fringe benefits, but $2,000,000 total on other expenses, your ratio is 1:2 compensation to non-compensation. If a ratio seems complicated to calculate, you can also view these totals as percentages of the operating budget. For example, $1,000,000 of salary expenses is approximately 33 percent of the overall operating budget of $3,000,000. As with most measures, there's no magic number or ratio you're trying to achieve, but a typical ratio will be around 1:2 (non-compensation is approximately twice that of compensation). Most importantly, the ratio can be used as a starting point for analysis and discussion. A ratio that's far out of balance can illustrate a few things. If the non-compensation figure is much higher than twice compensation, it may suggest that you're spending too much on supplies and services but not enough on staffing. This could imply that the staff is being overtaxed, because they're handling a lot of programmatic activity with a relatively small staff. Or you might be relying heavily on volunteers or lower-paid staff members.

If, on the other hand, the compensation amount is significantly out of proportion—for example, compensation is equal to or higher than non-compensation—it could suggest a lack of balance between staffing and activities. You may be over-staffed or may not have enough operating funds to support their activities. Your budget may feel perpetually crunched. Another potential issue indicated by a high compensation to non-compensation ratio may be high salaries, or executive salaries that are out of proportion for the institutional budget. As you can see, there's some nuance, and the ratio should be considered in the context of your museum's particular operating model. Does the ratio reveal what you thought it would? For example, if you feel your institution is understaffed, can you see evidence of that in the ratio? It's also very useful to pair this ratio with other benchmarking data, such as the staff size or operating budget of comparable institutions.

Assessing Activities

Another variation of the compensation/non-compensation ratio is to use it to assess spending for a particular activity. This is particularly useful to gain deeper insight into the museum's most complex, and often most expensive, budget items. The total should include both staffing and supplies and services for that particular activity or department. For example, in exhibitions, you would include all exhibition costs as well as any staff (or portion of positions) dedicated to exhibitions. This figure is particularly informative when comparing your operation and expenses to peer institutions.

This measure can sometimes reveal *how* you accomplish things. For example, at one institution, we had a relatively small staff compared to our peers. We knew this based on benchmarking studies and reviewing the staffing structures of comparable institutions. Yet, our exhibition spending (such as exhibition contracts, shipping, and supplies) was one of the highest in our peer group. Some additional analysis revealed that this was because we were bringing in more traveling exhibitions, which often carried a steep cost. We realized we were relying on outside exhibitions to shore up an undersized staff. This isn't necessarily problematic in itself. Sometimes it makes sense to pay for outside services. In this case, however, it had happened over time and wasn't necessarily a strategic decision. By looking at the department budget holistically, we realized that an increase in staffing could result in a decrease in temporary exhibition costs. Surprisingly, if we could convert supplies and services spending to staffing, there would be almost no impact at all on the overall exhibition budget.

Increasing the staff size and reducing costs for temporary exhibitions weren't the only positive outcomes to this shift. By investing in more staff members, rather than more outside temporary exhibitions, we were also able to better leverage our permanent collection and create more unique and regional exhibitions. The expanded staff could also better serve the public and answer research questions. Looking closely at the structure of spending in an activity or department, and comparing it to peers, can offer valuable insights. It's not always possible to easily convert supplies and services expenses to staffing support, or vice versa. But when it is, it makes sense to carefully analyze this ratio to understand the operating model it supports and consider strategic shifts.

Creating Comparisons

To get a better sense of where the organization puts its funding, you can also compare spending of sections or departments. For example, you can compare spending on education to spending on curatorial. For this exercise, it's helpful to include salaries as well as supplies and services for the section or department. You can also just use supplies and services spending if that's the figure readily available. Once you establish a consistent method, calculate the figures for each department, and then compare them to each other. There is again no "right" ratio here, but you might find it enlightening to see what the budget has to say about your strategic direction.

For example, I once worked in a museum where there was a lot of emphasis on expanding outreach and education. This had been in the strategic plan for years and was often the topic of discussion at advisory and planning meetings. Yet, when I ran this metric, the spending on curatorial outpaced education by three to one. Oops. This may reflect a lack of support behind a strategic direction. It may reflect the reality of a budget that has not yet caught up to where the institution is heading. It could even be "right sized," because the strategic priority doesn't actually require a lot of financial resources. More likely, however, the institution isn't actually putting its money where its mouth is, or is having trouble making measurable progress (that eagle is still soaring at ten thousand feet and hasn't come down to earth yet!). To gain more insight into this metric, it's helpful to pair it with other measures used to monitor the strategic initiatives. For example, if we had found that our outreach numbers were increasing year after year, this financial metric wouldn't have been so meaningful.

This is also a helpful ratio to monitor how sections and departments are evolving in an institution. If outreach and education is a priority in the strategic plan, then you would expect this section or department to expand over time. It can also show you where this growth is coming from. Unfortunately, money doesn't fall from the sky. If a department or activity has expanded, see if you can figure out how that growth is being supported. Is it because more revenue is coming in? Or are other sections (looking at you, administration) being cannibalized to create the momentum? This, again, isn't necessarily a problem as long as it's being done consciously. Growth of a department or activity may also be inadvertent or demonstrate unintentional creep (looking at you, administration).

If a section or department budget has expanded over time and it *wasn't* intentional, you might take some time to identify the reason. Are donor demands and restricted gifts actually steering the direction of the museum? Or are expenses just increasing due to factors outside of the museum's control, such as increasing costs for IT support? Or is one budget manager a little too good at advocating for resources at the expense of other departments? If growth wasn't intentional, it may need to be pulled back or brought back into proportion to other departments. This is where getting out of the weeds is essential. If you're managing a department budget, you may have no idea how your resources compare to those of other departments. Museum leadership needs to be aligning the budget at the institutional level and calling back to the strategic plan to make sure the two processes are in step.

Pinpointing Strategy

A related exercise is to take your strategic plan and map the initiatives and stated values to the budget. For example, your museum may identify accessibility as a strategic priority. Can you see that somewhere on your budget? Strategic priorities may not always be represented in dollar amounts, but it's difficult to move the needle if you're not actually putting resources behind your initiatives. If, for example, accessibility is a priority, how is that actually being implemented? Is it one of those "it's a part of everything we do" commitments with no resources actually behind it? Or are staff being expected to pick up these new initiatives in addition to their regular responsibilities? Or are strategic priorities displacing other activities (intentionally or otherwise)? What are the actual resources behind the strategic plan? If they're not represented on the budget in some way, they are less likely to succeed. This is again a particularly useful measure for monitoring change in your institution. If the institution is really advancing in its strategic direction, that should be represented somewhere in the budget. If you view the budget across time, there should be tangible evidence of this evolution.

It's difficult to have meaningful and sustainable change at an institution without it showing up on the budget.

Balanced Scorecard

Calculating ratios can be a useful exercise, but it's also beneficial to establish a more comprehensive and consistent method of tracking financial and non-financial data. While museums have become increasingly interested in evaluation, many institutions still lack a consistent way to monitor success against their strategic framework. A tool used in the business field is called a balanced scorecard.[1] The balanced scorecard creates a small group of metrics that help the organization create transparency and consistency in tracking. It's particularly valuable because it can include both financial and non-financial metrics and can be adapted to the particular culture and institution. It's also a great tool for creating insight into commitments that are harder to measure such as employee development and satisfaction. Financial measures are important but, used on their own, they can be misleading. For example, you may invest heavily in staff development resulting in a staff competent with current technology, knowledgeable about current trends, and satisfied in their jobs. Staff development comes at a financial cost, however, and the large expense might even look problematic if taken out of context. Yet, staff development is often a wise investment. This might be apparent when considering other perspectives, such as efficiency, employee satisfaction, or low turnover rates.

This balanced approach, of including both financial and non-financial metrics, makes the balanced scorecard particularly valuable for museums. While many of us recognize the need for museums to become more business-like, it can never be at the cost of our mission or public service. Sometimes this is a perceived barrier to instituting more stringent business policies. The balanced scorecard can integrate important indicators, such as customer satisfaction, with traditional financial measures, such as revenue generation. These perspectives are often siloed in museums, or education and outreach is overweighted at risk to the financial sustainability of the institution. In order to be successful, and sustainable, museums must do both.

The balanced scorecard focuses on four perspectives: (1) customer, (2) financial, (3) internal process, and (4) learning and development. These can be adapted as needed for your institution and its priorities. For example, you might decide to only use two perspectives or might add a new one of your own. The key though is balance. One of the strengths of the scorecard is that the perspectives are very different and complementary. Even within each perspective, you should try to identify measures that are balanced and insightful. There is room for traditional measures, such as quantifying attendance, but you might find that more creative measures can help the institution reframe success.

Sample Museum Strategic Plan

To demonstrate how these perspectives can come together into a balanced scorecard, I created a sample scorecard for a museum. To create meaningful measures, the balanced scorecard is grounded in the museum's strategic plan. My challenge was then to identify a small pool of metrics that would indicate progress toward these objectives. This museum's strategic plan focuses on three areas:

1. *Aligning Resources.* Evaluating staffing, funding, and partnerships to better support mission.
2. *Ensuring Sustainability.* Creating financial and programmatic sustainability to ensure the long-term success of the institution.
3. *Increasing Relevance.* Removing barriers to engagement through a renewed focus on visitor experience.

Creating a Balanced Scorecard

Customer Perspective

Of the four perspectives, the customer perspective is an obvious fit because of the public-facing mission of museums. The customer perspective relates to people who attend museum exhibitions and programs, which are often the cornerstone of the museum's public-facing mission. While visitor engagement is important in its own right, visitors can also become financial supporters through paid memberships, financial gifts, and even purchases at the museum store. You can see that the perspectives work together; when one area is successful it tends to filter over to other areas as well.

The customer perspective can be connected to the strategic plan in several ways. The one that stands out is the strategic commitment to increase relevance and remove barriers to engagement through a renewed focus on visitor experience. While not necessarily stated in the plan, a secondary effect would be increasing financial support through membership, gifts, and endowments. If this is the strategic direction, how can it be measured? One way is a simple measure of attendance. It's easy to measure and quantify attendance. But how can we measure engagement and the removal of barriers? The customer perspective could focus on two measures: attendance and the net promoter score.

Customer Perspective: Attendance

This is a quantitative measure of visitors who enter the museum and then enter various galleries and exhibitions. It indicates growth of the museum's overall visitation. This can also be used strategically to monitor, for example, the number of visitors to a particular exhibition, which indicates popularity and interest. Or it could be paired with demographic data to reach visitors from a particular region being reached through a new marketing campaign. It could also be used as the basis for a financially driven metric, such as visitors served/dollars spent per exhibition. This is a quantitative measure but, used in conjunction with the net promoter score, would indicate how many people are visiting and how satisfied they are with their experience.

- *Sample Target*: increase of 5 percent in attendance per year. Exhibition-focused attendance goals to be determined during exhibition planning.

Customer Perspective: Net Promoter Score

The net promoter score (NPS) is a measure of the quality of an experience, not the quantity of visitors. It can indicate how well the museum is engaging with visitors, and growing its fan base. An NPS is easy to administer. You can calculate an NPS using the answer to a key question, using a 0 to 10 scale: "How likely is it that you would recommend the museum to a friend or colleague?" Respondents are grouped as promoters (score 9–10), passives (score 7–8), or detractors (score 0–6). The NPS is then calculated by subtracting the percentage of detractors from the percentage of promoters. For example, if 75 percent of respondents are promoters, and 5 percent are detractors, the NPS is 70 percent.

- *Sample Target*: starting from a one-year baseline, improve rating by 5 percent annually.

Financial Perspective

The financial perspective is also an important consideration. While most museums are nonprofits, financial sustainability is a key indicator of success. Even large, well-funded museums can struggle with financial issues. Strategic management of resources is critical for success, and even survival. Some museums, such as large municipal institutions, operate much like a for-profit business with a significant percentage of revenue generated through areas such as admissions, concessions, and venue rentals. Others, typically those with stable government or foundation support, may offer free admission and limited concessions. All museums, however, need to manage resources effectively or they won't be able to fully achieve their public-facing mission.

Financial Perspective: Growth in Non-acquisition Endowment

Many art museums maintain two primary types of endowments: acquisition and non-acquisition. The acquisition endowment allows the museum to build its permanent art collection. The non-acquisition endowment may support programmatic activities such as exhibitions, public programs, marketing, and education. Growth in the non-acquisition endowment represents the potential for greater discretionary spending and the addition of permanent positions. The endowment is a steady source of income, even in uncertain times, and can help balance out variance in annual giving trends. This measure assesses growth as a percentage of the previous year. Growth is dependent on market factors, which are outside of the museum's control, but also additions to the endowment that are secured by development.

- *Sample Target*: increase of 1 percent per year, may be averaged over three years.

Financial Perspective: Programming as Percentage of Total Operating Budget

Monitoring the percentage of the total operating budget helps the museum assess how much of its budget supports mission-specific activities. This helps the museum ensure that an appropriate percentage of its operating budget supports public-facing programs and keeps administrative and supporting expenses in line. This measure might be selected by a museum committed to growing and sustaining its outreach efforts. As the overall budget grows, the amount invested in outreach should also keep pace.

- *Sample Target*: at least 25 percent of operating costs dedicated to public programs and exhibitions.

Learning and Growth Perspective

The learning and development perspective often refers to staff professional development, either in their own areas or how they come together to learn and grow as a staff. For example, this may include developing skills and communication around diversity, equity, and accessibility initiatives. Or it could represent travel, conference attendance, and degree progression. It can also include learning and development related to an internal system, such as new project management software or a parent agency's financial system. By building learning and development into the balanced scorecard, it acknowledges that staff development is a valuable investment. If museum staff members don't have opportunities to develop and grow, and don't feel valued and supported, the museum itself will also stagnate. Staff development is a true financial investment, and a mutual benefit, not just a perk of employment.

Learning and Growth Perspective: Training Investment Compared to Staffing Budget

While some training opportunities are low-cost, this metric allows the museum to track the resource investment in staff training and development. As the staff grows, and salaries hopefully grow, the investment grows larger to provide additional opportunities and equitable distribution of resources.

- *Sample Target*: at least $1 spent on training for each $100 on staffing (e.g., $15,000 spent on training for a $1,500,000 staffing budget).

Learning and Growth Perspective: Number of Professional Outreach Initiatives per Year

The strategic initiative to increase relevance also applies to the museum's professional standing within the field. The museum supports staff opportunities to contribute through conference presentations, professional papers, innovative exhibitions and programs, and professional publications. This metric quantifies this type of outreach and also may reflect when internal demands interfere with this objective. By identifying this as an institution-wide measure, it may also encourage development of panel presentations with a representation of individuals from across the institution.

- *Sample Target*: at least three outreach initiatives per year.

Internal Process

The internal process perspective is one that is often overlooked in museums, and many other organizations, but attention to this area offers the potential for greater employee satisfaction, efficiency, and communication. For example, if you find that the exhibition development process is confusing and cumbersome, it's probably a process issue. If invoices take forever to get paid or you get calls from frustrated vendors, the process could use improvement. The internal process perspective may relate to the organization and growth of the museum staff. For example, departments might be siloed and might benefit from a restructuring to promote collaboration. Identifying areas for improvement in internal processes can help the museum run more efficiently, which improves the operation as well as the financial situation.

Internal Process: Establish a Clear Contract Review Process

Museums may need to solicit a significant amount of input into exhibition, and other legal, contracts. Mistakes or oversights can be costly or create legal liability. A clear review process will identify the staff members who need to provide input and assign responsibility for routing contracts. A clear process will improve efficiency and reduce the time to review and finalize contracts. This type of measure may only remain on the balanced scorecard until it's achieved, at which time a new measure can be established for this perspective.

- *Sample Target*: establish a clear contract review process.

Internal Process: Number of Business Days to Process Invoices

The speed of invoice processing reflects efficiency of administration. Paying invoices promptly also helps safeguard relationships with artists, galleries, and suppliers. Improving the speed of processing may require an improved process and allows a way to check in on it to be sure it's maintained. Often when these types of processes break down, the reasons are complex. For example, staff members may be hanging on to invoices for too long. Administrative staff may need more training on procedure. Or, for museums with parent agencies, invoices may be stalling out at levels above the museum. This type of measure is a small window into the overall administration of the museum.

- *Sample Target*: 95 percent of invoices processed within five business days of receipt.

You can see that the balanced scorecard is incredibly flexible. It can create a useful mix of measures that relate not only to the visitor experience but also to financial sustainability as well as staff development. The museum field has made significant advancements in visitor evaluation but may overlook staff satisfaction and financial development. By combining these into one concise scorecard, a handful of metrics can help the museum and its stakeholders quickly check in. One of the strengths of the scorecard is that it can easily be adapted to a range of institutions and can change over time as the museum itself evolves. The balanced scorecard shows significant potential for use in the museum field and other nonprofit industries.

Snooping on Your Neighbors

As you get more comfortable with budgets, you'll benefit from occasionally looking over the financial reports of your own institution as well as those of peer museums. You can easily find museum budget documents and financial reports published online. You'll learn a lot by looking at financial reports of institutions that are similar to your own to see how they bring in revenue and what they spend it on. You'll learn even more by looking at financial reports of institutions that are nothing like your own! For example, I work in a university museum and find it fascinating to occasionally look over the financial reports of municipal museums. So much is the same, but there are important differences too. For example, they might have revenue-generating programs that we never even considered. Or they might mention granting agencies that we haven't engaged with yet. Don't be afraid to look around and see what you can learn. I wouldn't recommend starting with the report of a very large institution because they're complex, although if you're feeling brave you should jump right in. No matter how complicated, nearly every financial report will include the same basic components: revenue and expenses.

As you look over financial reports, you'll notice a few things. One is that they are based on things that have already occurred—in other words, they are typically based on accounting not budgeting. So, you'll only see figures on revenue that the museum actually brought in (it may not be the revenue that they had hoped to bring in) and figures on expenses that the museum actually incurred (it may not be what they thought they would spend). While the report might look polished and the planning looks perfectly accurate, there's probably more to the story. Another thing to keep in mind is that published financial reports may also only represent a single year. So, it can provide a snapshot in time but it may not represent the museum's overall financial position. Some museums may publish information for multiple years which is a helpful way to understand trends. Despite the limitations of publicly available information, learning from your neighbors can be enlightening and help you better understand the structure and priorities at your own institution.

If you're new to budgeting, you might find a financial report a bit overwhelming. To begin, just look it over, see if anything stands out to you. Look at each line and see if you can understand what it represents. Don't worry about trying to understand every detail. Look for the larger trends or indicators. Here are some questions you might consider when reviewing a financial report:

- When looking at the revenue, can you tell where it comes from? What is the largest category of revenue?
- When looking at expenses, where does the institution spend the most money? How does it categorize its expenses? By program, by section, by activity?
- Where does the institution spend the most money? The least money? Do these categories seem to align with their strategic initiatives?
- If you have access to multi-year reports, see if you can identify any obvious trends.

As you advance in your knowledge and confidence, you might ask more complex questions. If you're fortunate enough to have a budget or financial specialist on staff at your institution, they may be willing to help you develop a better understanding of your institution's budget. If you don't have a specialist on staff, or they're not able to help, you can teach yourself. Much of this information can be found in annual reports. Instead of reading the glossy summary at the front, flip to the middle or back of the report to get to the good stuff.

If there are any significant anomalies from year to year, it can be interesting to identify the cause. This may be provided in the supporting narrative, or you may have to do your own detective work. The idea is not to be critical of another museum's operation but to understand how non-financial issues can surface in financial ways. For example, I was recently looking at budget information for a small group of peer universities. One of them had incredibly high spending in a particular area, but only for one year. A little research revealed that they had paid a large legal settlement in that year. If you didn't have that context, you might believe that their expenses were way out of line compared to peer institutions. But in reality, it was a one-time event that had no bearing on larger budget trends.

Continuing to Learn from Your Numbers

The above examples illustrate how you can glean valuable insights from your budgets and financial reports. Budgets are "strategy in action" and it can be useful to get beyond the numbers to better understand what they represent. There are numerous other metrics, dashboards, and exercises you can create at your institution. Often, the most valuable part of analysis is the discussion and reframing that surrounds it. Budgets left on a shelf can be lifeless documents, so don't be afraid to play around with the numbers to see what you can discover.

Three Ways to Expand Your Financial Knowledge:

1. Go online and find an annual report for a museum similar to your own. Does it appear that the museum has enough funding to cover expenses? Is there a surplus or deficit represented?

2. What are some of the budget challenges the institution is facing? You might find supporting information in the report narrative.
3. What is the budgeting process like? Can you tell who's involved and how are decisions made? Who is the report addressed to?

Note

1. Robert S. Kaplan and David P. Norton, "The Balanced Scorecard: Measures That Drive Performance," *Harvard Business Review*, August 1, 2014. https://hbr.org/1992/01/the-balanced-scorecard-measures-that-drive-performance-2.

11

Shaking the Piggy Bank

Whether due to internal growth or external pressures, most museums will encounter financial challenges and limitations. There are traditionally only two ways to increase financial sustainability: increasing revenue or reducing expenses. While budgeting often focuses on expenses, reducing spending can only take you so far. And for many institutions, increasing revenue is also a difficult proposal. So, it's important to maximize available revenue and use it efficiently. This includes making careful decisions about how to leverage it and what initiatives it should support. Aside from the obvious steps of implementing solid budgeting and fiscal oversight, there are some additional things you can do to make the most of your revenue.

Fund Reviews

Sometimes increasing revenue doesn't require more funding, it just requires more flexibility with the funds you already have. For this reason, if you manage funds at your institution, I highly recommend conducting a regular fund review. A fund review involves a careful look at the terms, conditions, and use of each institutional fund. This might involve, for example, going through the paperwork of each gift and endowment fund to read the original terms and conditions and verify how you're using it. A fund review often provides insight into fund restrictions. You might learn that a fund you thought was restricted is actually discretionary. Or the way a fund has been used historically became misunderstood as a restriction rather than a preference. This might be surprising, but even a medium-sized art museum can have fifty to a hundred gift or endowment funds to manage. Some might have been established decades ago and the terms of the fund might have been transcribed from paper to digital format along the way. Over time, restrictions can become misinterpreted or represent only a snippet of a fuller document. Reviewing the fund terms and conditions can also remind you of the donor's original intent, which may create additional opportunities for stewardship and acknowledgment.

A fund review is important for many reasons, but one is shaking up the piggy bank to make sure you're using all of your resources effectively. If you're fortunate, a fund review can open up some additional funding. If you're not, you may find that the restrictions on an old fund were more detailed than you realized, and you can make adjustments. Either way, it's a good idea to verify the original restriction on a periodic basis so the funds are used as effectively and as appropriately as possible. This is particularly helpful during a leadership transition so that the new director, or department head, has a clear understanding of the funds that are available for use and any restrictions on those funds. It's also a good time to consider closing fully expended funds, combining funds where possible, or making decisions about whether to reinvest endowment income.

In addition to reviewing terms and conditions, a fund review can include a thorough analysis of how a fund is being used and if it's being effectively leveraged. If you have a restricted fund, for example, you might find that it's not used very often. This may be because key staff members are unaware of it or because the fund is so tightly restricted. Depending on the policies that govern your funds, you may be able to appeal this restriction or request some allowances from the original donor. During a recent fund review, our institution was able to free up more than $100,000 annually. This included better use of several funds, including one where the restriction needed more clarification and one that had been established long ago to support a program that no longer existed. By making a case to our supporting foundation, they were able to carefully consider the donor intent and release the funds for a slightly broader use. These funds then became a source of vital support for the museum and are now frequently used. While donors may have specific requests for how their funds are used, and those must be respected, no one benefits when gifts are not fully leveraged. You can benefit your institution as well as your donors when you conduct a fund review on a regular basis. A fund review also opens up communication between the people who use the funds and those who manage them. This helps promote transparency and communication and contributes to a culture of strong financial management.

While fund reviews are most relevant to museums with endowments and gifts, they're also useful for smaller museums that may operate on only one or two sources of funding. For example, you might find that one of your two funds rolls over from year to year, while the other doesn't. In that case, you would prioritize the use of the fund that would lapse back at the end of the year. Or you might discover that a fund provided by a parent agency has more flexibility (or more restrictions) than you realize. Regardless of your particular situation, it's always an advantage to gain a greater understanding of how your funds are structured and can be optimized.

Learning to Say No, or Not Yet

One of the best ways to manage resources effectively is to use them in focused ways to achieve your mission and vision. Even the most well-funded museum doesn't have unlimited resources. When you have a strong strategic planning and budgeting framework, it can help you identify your highest priorities and aspirational initiatives. It can also help you avoid the common pitfall of creating a program or activity around a source of available funding, rather than finding available funding for your actual institutional priorities. This is a common issue because resources are in short supply. Everyone wants to land that major grant, or please an important donor. There is a real danger, however, in going astray if funding opportunities lead programming rather than vice versa.

If you've worked in the museum or nonprofit field for a while, you've probably witnessed a case of people saying yes, when maybe they should have said no. This happens in all areas of museums. For example, an important donor offers a piece of artwork that the museum would normally decline. They accept it in order to retain goodwill with the individual. Or a stakeholder offers to fund a public program that the museum was planning to discontinue because it no longer seems relevant to the mission. The museum accepts the gift and continues the program rather than potentially alienating the individual. This might be a strategic decision, with good reasons behind it, but it comes at a cost. This also happens in the world of museum finance and development. The most common scenario is that a donor offers a financial gift, but it comes with heavy restrictions. Maybe they want the funding to be used for a very specific activity, something that's not even in the museum's operational or strategic plan. Saying no may cause hard feelings and could result in losing the gift. Saying yes may cause a strain on the museum staff and a drift of the museum's mission. Or the funding may be accepted but sit unused year after year. A colleague once told me that her answer in that situation was never "no," it was "not yet." That wouldn't work in every situation, of course, but it can be a way to continue the conversation without damaging a relationship with a museum supporter. Depending on the donor or funding agency, this can also be a good opportunity to draw them into your vision and discuss your institutional priorities.

The tendency to say yes when you should say no can also happen with grant opportunities. Have you ever read a grant announcement and wondered what project you could create in order to land the funding? I've done this too, but it's pretty strange when you think about it. We're creating more work, in order to land funding that we don't currently need, in order to take on a project we didn't know we wanted to do. Why we do this? Maybe it's because budgets aren't about numbers. Landing a major grant might result in publicity for the museum, it may create an exciting new initiative, it could be something to highlight at a board meeting or on a performance review. It's satisfying to take on a project with a clear timeline and measurable outcomes. It feels like forward momentum, but it's not actually progress unless it connects back to the priorities. The frequent mismatch between strategic planning and budgeting is also why a new grant or donor funded initiative may be so tempting even when it's not right for the organization. We get drawn in by the priorities of the funding institution or the donor, instead of staying committed to our own. The expected outcomes might be exaggerated ("this is going to be amazing!") and the internal work minimized ("although we're understaffed, we'll handle it somehow"). The new project is neatly paired with fresh resources. There might be a reporting requirement or outside accountability that keeps things on track. This makes it (seem) easier to accomplish than internal initiatives, which might require that other activities have to be reprioritized or sacrificed.

Creating a Wish List

In order to try to avoid this situation but still leverage grant and other funding opportunities, you can create a wish list of projects and initiatives for your institution. These will often be guided by the strategic plan and are primarily projects limited only by a lack of funding or other resources. If time allows, you can even create short narratives and working budgets for some of the initiatives. Creating a narrative about the project allows you to clearly outline the reasons for undertaking them and also allows you to respond more quickly when funding opportunities present themselves. Perhaps, most importantly, they become the highest-priority initiatives for the institution. If you're tempted to pursue funding or accept a gift for a project not on your wish list, you'll need to take a hard look at the justification. This will help you stay the course and not get distracted by new strategic directions.

This approach of creating a short narrative and working budget isn't only for new initiatives. It can also work well for fundable activities that you're already doing. For example, as a university museum, we employ several graduate students every year. These positions include a fair wage, benefits, and tuition remission, so they're fairly expensive for the museum. But they provide excellent experience for the graduate students, while bringing their valuable perspectives into our planning and programming. We believed this area would be a great funding opportunity, so we had developed a short paragraph about the benefits and budget for the positions. We had submitted it for one funding opportunity but, unfortunately, it was declined. We filed away the supporting narrative and budget information for future use.

Not long after this occurred, we had a call out of the blue from an individual who admired the museum and was interested in making a gift made possible by an estate situation. We were able to quickly forward our existing narrative and budget, and she generously agreed to fund the graduate students for the coming year! She also commented that she had talked to other museums as well and we were the first to get back to her with a concrete proposal. This was the beginning of a new relationship with this donor. She has become more engaged with the museum, enjoys receiving updates about the graduate students, and has continued to provide generous support in subsequent years. It's rare that a new supporter will call us out of the blue, but funding support can come from a variety of places. If you're ready, you'll be well-prepared to take advantage of them and be able to demonstrate that you have solid planning in place. So, get your wish list ready and you might find that opportunities come your way sooner than you expect. And most importantly, you're leading with mission and vision, not funding.

In addition to establishing your funding priorities, I also recommend keeping a file with narrative snippets about the museum such as the mission, vision, facility, and history. These don't change that often, so they can be easily plugged into grant or funding proposals without re-writing them each time. Most grant applications and donor proposals have commonalities, so you don't necessarily have to start from scratch. This can make the process more efficient, and you can fine-tune these narrative sections over time. I also do this with paragraphs that don't make the final cut of a particular proposal, or even full proposals that weren't successful. I just file them into a working Word document and pull them out for other uses. It's also worth the time to create a polished and compelling description of the museum and its priorities. This is an investment in itself. This can often be done with a public relations firm but can also be created internally if you don't have resources for outside assistance. This should be a short, descriptive, and compelling blurb about the museum. Once you have it written, you'll find multiple uses for it. It can easily fit into grant applications, as well as job postings, press releases, and other material. By spending some on it in advance, you'll create a polished and professional foundation for competitive funding applications or donor proposals.

Bang for Your Buck

Unless you're in the enviable position of having more funding than you need, your museum will need to make difficult decisions about priorities. There are numerous ways to assess the value and cost of programming decisions. We do this informally all of the time, but it's worth taking the time to assess initiatives with a more structured process. This is easier to do for potential projects but even more valuable for existing ones.

First, be clear about what the initiative is supposed to accomplish. Is it mostly to generate revenue? Or is it primarily for outreach? There are often multiple benefits, and you can use a simple rating matrix. You can start by first listing the primary goals and the necessary factors. Examples might include potential for revenue generation: increasing awareness; supportable with current staffing or financial capacity; geographical or demographic reach; connection to mission.

These are just examples and will vary by the type of activity you're planning. For example, if you're committed to free public programs, potential for revenue generation may not even be on your list. If your goal is to raise funds, then revenue might be primary but increasing awareness could also be important. Once you have a short list of the important factors, you can weight or rank them. For example, on a scale of 0 to 3, revenue generation might be a "3," or most important, while increasing awareness might be a "2," important, but not as important as revenue.

For nearly all initiatives, you'll probably want to include connection to mission as one of the factors. Your primary goal might be revenue, for example, but the initiative should also support, or at least not conflict with, your mission and vision. All other things equal, an initiative that does this would be more appealing than one that doesn't. It can also help you recognize when revenue programs don't connect well to the mission. If they don't, then you may want to consider options to modify them. For example, rental programs are often very profitable for museums. Can you modify the program to also advance the mission? Could you provide tours to event attendees, distribute membership information, or have a curator give a talk?

I also recommend including a factor relating to cost, for example, manageable with existing staff capacity and funding. This is important because it creates a check on ideas. You can dream up an amazing program that will bring in thousands of attendees but may not have the capacity to implement it. So, the criteria should include what you want to achieve, but also the factors or limitations that would make an initiative successful. If you do conduct this exercise for a new project, I highly recommend assessing and weighting your criteria in advance before any ideas are shared. Otherwise, you might find that your criteria are skewed by the projects already on the table.

Once you have your criteria in place, you can brainstorm potential projects, then score them in each factor. You can again use a simple 0-1-2-3 rating scale. After scoring each initiative in each factor, you would then multiply the score of each factor by the weight you previously assigned. For example, a museum might be interested in a program that increases awareness and has a connection to mission. They don't need to generate revenue but do want it to be affordable and manageable for their staff. They weighted increasing awareness as a "3" (most important consideration), connection to mission a "3," and available capacity (staff and funding) a "2" (moderately important).

One of their ideas is to create a speakers bureau and have staff members travel to provide presentations to community groups for a small fee. The program will create awareness, although staff limitations mean they will only reach a relatively small number of people. So, in increasing awareness, they scored it as a 2. Then they multiply the score (2) by the weight of this factor, which is 3. So, in increasing awareness, this initiative scores a 6 (2 x 3). The initiative connects very well to the mission, so it scores a 3, or a weighted 9. They have the staff capacity to undertake it, and it's not very costly, so it also scores a 3 on this factor. This factor was weighted as a 2 (moderately important), for a weighted score of 6. If you add all of the weighted scores together, this initiative scores 21, out of a potential score of 24. The total score should represent how well it achieves the museum's priorities. They could then repeat the exercise for other ideas they're considering.

One thing I really like about this exercise is that it's (somewhat) objective. You might come up with a really interesting idea but find that, in the end, the rating shows that it won't meet your objectives. Maybe revenue generation is rated as an important factor, but the program is all flash and no cash! Or you might have a "sleeper," an idea that doesn't seem that exciting initially, but it scores high in the overall criteria. It can also help you compare objectives against one another to determine their strengths and weaknesses, and how they might complement your existing programs. For example, if you have a wildly popular public program that doesn't generate any revenue, you might want to put your focus on creating other programs that do. Once you isolate the factors that are important to the museum, it's easier to understand what a program does or doesn't do well.

This exercise is also a great way to facilitate discussion and communication. For example, I used this format to help plan a new outreach program with a partner institution. Before throwing out any ideas, we first determined our priorities as a group and assigned them weights. And then we listed all of our ideas on a whiteboard and scored them against the criteria. We ended up with a great outreach idea and it wasn't one that was an early front-runner. But when we scored and assessed the initiatives against our priorities, we realized it was the idea that best achieved goals. It was implemented and turned out to be very successful and long-lasting. Even more important, however, was the discussion around what was important and manageable for both institutions.

Taking time to objectively evaluate ideas can also help ensure that more voices are heard when it comes to resource management decisions. Often, an idea is championed by one or two individuals who are the most outspoken or have the most influence in the group. By asking the team to discuss and arrive at ratings together, it gives everyone a chance to participate and all ideas a chance. It also helps avoid the tendency of groups to move forward with the first idea or the most creative one, which is not always the best one. Consider *what* you want your resources to achieve before you identify the specific vehicle for achieving it.

The Myth of Being Saved by the Museum Store

Museums often struggle with funding and look for new ways to support their operation and mission-based activities. There are numerous ways to create additional funding streams or shore up your existing ones. Earned revenue initiatives should be assessed carefully, however, and with an eye to their true revenue potential, as well as how they relate to your mission and capacity. Many museums run a store, for example, so there is a common assumption that stores generate money. Well, they do. Sometimes. Stores also lose money! And the true cost can be camouflaged if you're not looking carefully enough.

Almost no program is free because there's always an investment of some kind. Whether it's the purchase of new supplies or fixtures, the time of staff members, or the effort to organize and manage volunteers, nearly every earned revenue or development initiative has a cost. As nonprofit institutions, we often overlook the investment of staff time and resources spent on fundraising or programming initiatives.

As you assess earned revenue initiatives, also be wary about being overly optimistic with your planning assumptions. Is it really feasible to manage a museum store with volunteers? Will volunteers be proactive about sales and customer service? Can someone cover if a volunteer or part-time employee doesn't show up? If your assumptions are wrong, what would the worst-case scenario look like? What is your Plan B? And, most importantly, who will be responsible for assessing the program and correcting course if it's needed?

Especially for earned revenue initiatives, it's essential to create a pro forma budget to assess the costs and expected revenue. For a typical earned revenue initiative, this might include expected sales, cost of goods sold, staffing, and associated administrative costs such as marketing, inventory systems, or shipping costs. Do your best to ground your planning in reality by talking to peer institutions and working with professional organizations to obtain data and reports about comparable initiatives. These organizations and reports can also help you set realistic expectations. For example, if you're considering a museum store, they can provide typical sales per customer or sales per square foot.

In my experience, museum stores do well when the institution is fully committed and ready to invest in professional staffing and administrative support. In short, when they're run like a business. Museums may also generate some revenue from a volunteer-based retail program, but the cost-benefit analysis usually shows the program takes as much to run as it generates. So, proceed carefully. If revenue is your goal, then it's worth brainstorming other ideas which may have a lower cost and commitment.

Go Big, and Then Go Home

In a previous museum, I witnessed what it's like to forget the goal of an initiative and get caught up in overly optimistic budget projections. We had a stakeholder who was a local celebrity and he wanted to help us plan a fundraising gala. The idea of a gala was new for our institution, so we didn't have a realistic sense of what it would cost or what we could raise. It was exciting though. Our supporter had been involved with similar events and told us to go big! He kept suggesting features and amenities. Soon we had rented an expensive event hall, booked several musical acts, and agreed to an elaborate menu. I think we had a chocolate fountain (they were a thing at the time). While we were selling a lot of tickets, we were giving away a lot, too. The event organizer had a working budget, but it could barely keep up with all of the changes that were being made. And, of course, it was difficult to project revenue because it was the first time that we had held this type of event.

The event was a success in many ways. Everyone seemed to have a fun night, we created new awareness, and even gained some new members. People were dancing to a big band until the early morning. Whoo. Unfortunately, though, after the excitement of the event faded, we realized that it wasn't a success in one important way: revenue. After closing the books and processing the final invoices, we came to the sad conclusion that we had actually lost money. On a fundraising event. That we had spent hundreds of staff hours on. This was a difficult lesson in realistic budgeting and in setting clear priorities. While creating awareness of the museum was important, we forgot that the primary reason for the event was to generate revenue. If every decision had to relate back to that priority, we would have made very different choices.

It also taught us the importance of controlling decisions that create consequences for the museum. That probably sounds obvious, but it was easy to get caught up in an exciting plan. An exciting plan crafted by someone who didn't have to pay the bills. No one came to bail us out after the event was over, and we never told the donor that we lost money. He had good intentions, so I'm sure he would have been horrified. It was an expensive lesson, but we took time to reflect on what went wrong so it never happened again.

Donors aren't the only well-meaning stakeholders who can egg you on to poor decisions. Vendors can also overpromise, allow the scope to creep, or encourage you to spend more than you should. This can often happen with tech projects, for example, where you become so caught up that you forget what you are even trying to accomplish. I call it being distracted by "something shiny." Is your *goal* to have the most current technology in the galleries? Or is that just one possible vehicle for your goal, which is to provide visitors with engaging and educational information about the exhibit? Sometimes vendors even come disguised as nonprofits, who really just want to "help" your organization (always with a substantial contribution of your time and money). They might actually want to help, and the project might even be successful, but be cautious. Outside stakeholders will usually disappear as soon as the final check is written. You'll be the one left trying to explain what went wrong and why so many resources were invested in a lackluster outcome.

Hoarding: The Budget Episode

Effective resource management is all about planning for how to use funds so that they're leveraged effectively but not overspent. Not surprisingly, we spent most of this time worrying about not going over budget. These are the stories that make the news. We frequently hear of large projects failing because they were over budget or poorly managed. There are numerous stories about museums struggling financially and even closing because of budget management. Yet, an equally serious problem is *under*spending, it just doesn't make headlines. But if a museum is leaving funds on the table, it's not accomplishing everything it could. Usually, this isn't an intentional decision but one that comes out of issues with budget management and communication.

A new budget manager sometimes believes the worst thing that can possibly happen is coming in over budget. One reaction to this fear is to overestimate expenses so drastically that there's little chance of ever going over budget. There's nothing wrong with building in a small contingency for unexpected expenses. This is a legitimate budgeting technique that can provide flexibility. This is more than building in a contingency, however. I think of it more like resource hoarding, which involves drastic inflation of a budget even when it's clear that the funds will not be used or needed. I have witnessed this at multiple institutions and with staff members from all backgrounds. This is usually well-intentioned, but resource hoarding carries a lot of implications for the institutional budget. First, it inflates the overall budget projection so that administrators may inaccurately estimate how much revenue is needed. This may cause unneeded stress about the financial stability of the institution. More importantly, it locks up resources that then can't be used in other areas. This can result in strategic initiatives being put on hold, other important projects being delayed, and even basic needs such as building maintenance being paused. In some institutions, if funding is not spent by the end of the period, it may even be completely lost if it can't be rolled over. In other cases, the institution may have to go back to a donor or granting agency and explain why the funds they requested weren't actually used. If the institution is paying attention, this will show up halfway through the year, which then creates the need to reshuffle and reallocate funds. If the institution doesn't spot it, then they may end the fiscal year with a large surplus. Sometimes the budget manager is proud that they "saved" money, unaware of the ripple effect their planning has caused. A small deficit is almost always better than a large surplus.

Other than the fear of going over budget or poor planning, there are other reasons for resource hoarding. And not surprisingly, they're not about money. Funding demonstrates value. Section budget managers may feel that a large budget demonstrates how important their program is to the institution. This is also a way of advocating for their section. It can also be a cover for larger issues with strategic planning. A growing budget suggests progress. It can be impressive to present an ambitious budget request for the year. Removing an item from the budget later is a tangible admission that it won't get accomplished that year after all. Budget managers may also worry that a reduction in any given year may result in a more permanent decrease to their budget in future years. This can frequently occur in institutions where resources are scarce and competition is high.

Transparency is an important tool to build trust and confidence. If budget managers are grabbing a large piece of the pie, it may be because they don't have a good understanding of the financial situation of the museum. They may be zoomed in too tightly on their own section, department, or activity, either because that information is not being shared or because they need to step back to see the larger picture. They may also need to trust the institution and the people who distribute resources. If they're concerned that they won't receive funding they need to accomplish their strategic initiatives, they might just grab resources where they can. Budget managers who work as a team learn to be supportive of each other's success. Probably most importantly, they will learn to trust themselves and their own planning. They need to be realistic about what they can accomplish in a year and support their plans with a realistic request for resources. Often, after a few years of managing a budget, this tendency will lessen as they get to know their capacity and costs better. As they become more invested in budgeting, they may also learn to set aside time and energy for sufficient planning (both financial and operational).

This is also a situation where quarterly reviews become so vital. Frequent conversation and review will help a budget manager identify issues before they become too difficult to overcome. At each quarter, they'll have an opportunity to review their planning work and make adjustments if necessary. It also gives the overall budget manager a bird's-eye view on how the institution is managing its resources. There needs to be a strong sense of trust in budget discussions. Otherwise, you can drive issues underground and budget managers will try to hide them or be reluctant to talk about them. Then they end the year with a big surplus (or big deficit) which seems like a surprise. Any *serious* budget issues with a particular budget manager should be discussed in private, not in front of a group. And nearly all issues should be approached with a spirit of understanding and education.

This extends to being open and honest at all levels of the institution. For example, I manage one of our section budgets, and I try to be transparent about my own budget projections. If I have a small projected deficit/variance, I just leave it on the books and explain it during a budget discussion. In this way, I try to demonstrate that small deficits aren't an issue, and that my planning also isn't perfect. I explain what went into my planning assumption and what has changed, and how I might learn from it for future planning.

These techniques can help you leverage your existing resources and develop new ones, so they can best support your institutional mission and vision. Sometimes resource management requires hard choices, but no museum can do it all. By taking the time to conduct a fund review, assess programming decisions, and build trust in the budgeting process, we can use our limited resources as effectively as possible.

Three Ways to Expand Your Financial Knowledge:

1. Review any earned revenue initiatives at your museum. Can you see the connection to the museum's mission?
2. Choose one fund to focus on and learn more about. If you don't have access to the financial information or original terms and conditions, you might still be able to learn about the fund's purpose and what type of activities it supports.
3. Begin to develop a brief narrative and working budget for a project you'd like to pursue.

12

✛

Restoring Balance

At some point in your career, you may find yourself facing a difficult financial situation, even a large budget deficit or outstanding debt. You may have inherited the situation, or even unwittingly played a role in creating it. Or it could be due to circumstances that were truly unforeseeable. This isn't unusual in museums, unfortunately, but it's important to address financial issues before they snowball and become worse. Addressing a deficit or debt can be difficult and daunting, but there are steps you can take to minimize the damage and restore financial sustainability.

If you have experience with disaster response, you might find these concepts familiar. You can't handle everything at once and it's easy to become over-whelmed. So a more manageable approach is triaging the situation and address-ing the most urgent issues first, figuring out what happened, and then putting systems in place to help ensure it doesn't happen again.

- *Step 1: Stop the leak.* What's the cause of the deficit or debt? Was it a one-time issue? Is it still continuing? Is it a horrifying snowball that's getting larger and larger? If your financial management has been loose, you may need to spend some time on this step to understand the root cause. You may need outside assistance. For this initial analysis, you don't need to get too far into the weeds, however. Just try to identify the major causes. Often, they relate to a single (big) bad decision. They can also sneak up, however, and relate to routine overspending or a lack of a structured budget review process.
- *Step 2: Communicate.* Alert the people who need to know (if they don't already). You now know what caused the issue, so you can have an honest discussion with the people who need to know about it. For example, if the museum director has not been actively engaged with the budget, he or she obviously needs to know. If you're the director, you may need to alert your parent agency or the museum board. You may also need to have an honest conversation with staff members, based on the impact of the situation and

their relative need to know. You may also choose to wait until you establish a reduction plan and can present the solution along with the problem.

- *Step 3: Mitigation.* Here, you'll assess the immediate needs of the institution. For example, make sure that no bills are outstanding or that there are no looming obligations that need to take priority. Basic needs such as rent, utilities, and salaries will take priority. Do your best to clean up any damage that was done, such as vendors who may be reluctant to work with your organization.
- *Step 4: Determine your strategy.* When dealing with a deficit or debt, there are only two ways out. Reduce funding or increase revenue. Or both. In most cases, you have more control over expenses. While you might be able to increase revenue to support expenses, asking for assistance with debt reduction isn't a very appealing case. So, you'll probably need to figure out how to trim your budget instead. It might require pulling back severely on discretionary expenses for a few years. The baseline budgeting exercise in this book may be useful in this situation. Review your budgeting to determine approximately how much you can reduce spending (or increase revenue) on an annual basis. If you don't have a working budget already, then you'll need to start there before you can get a handle on things.
- *Step 5: Create a reduction plan.* Now you can create a plan for reduction. Calculate or review the deficit number. Don't be afraid. Using the annual amount that you identified in step 4, you can divide the deficit by that annual amount and create an idea of how long it will take you to eliminate the deficit. If it's debt and you're paying interest, that will also have to be factored in. If it's a multi-year plan, you can set interim goals to keep yourself on track and the institution accountable. Be sure the plan is well-documented and reviewed frequently. This will be helpful if others eventually have to manage the deficit, or if questions arise about how it's being handled. It also gives you some protection because it documents your awareness and responsibility. You can't change the past, but you can actively address the situation.
- *Step 6: Implement safeguards.* As you put together a plan and communicate with those who need to know, it's important to put safeguards in place for the future. If you spent some time identifying the cause of the deficit, you should have some clues that will alert you to trouble in the future. For example, you may need a more stringent budget process, you might need outside support, or you may need to reduce expenses or increase funding on a permanent basis. Implementing safeguards will not only lessen the likelihood of a similar situation occurring in the future, it will make deficit reduction more effective because you'll be better at managing the limited funds you do have.
- *Step 7: Resolve the deficit or debt.* Take a deep breath, celebrate a little, and continue to get your financial house in order. Go back to step 1 to more fully analyze what happened and why.

Exercise: Baseline Budgeting

An exercise that is useful in challenging financial situations is called "baseline budgeting." Even if you don't face financial difficulties, you might find it valuable to assess which expenses are truly necessary ("baseline") and which are more discretionary. You don't have to be in a financial crisis to conduct this exercise. In fact, I would recommend running through it at least once before you actually need it. You'll find that some of your planning has to be modified to the particular situation (a global pandemic wasn't on my list), but it's still useful to have a sense of what your institution actually needs to survive. This can also be a helpful way to plan for budget shortfalls. We plan for building evacuations and water main breaks, and we can also plan for budget disasters. Finally, it can help you focus on what is truly necessary and important to your mission and vision. This is helpful for creating clarity, even if you never experience a budget reduction.

This exercise will give you the approximate cost to operate your institution and keep it afloat, over the short and long term. This is a "no frills" budget, which may not achieve your institutional priorities or move you ahead but, rather, keep you alive to fight another day. You can also use this exercise as a quick way to review a section or program rather than larger institutional budgets. You will need a financial report, or least a planning budget for this exercise. When I conduct a baseline budgeting exercise, I consider the following categories. As you work through the categories, you might find that you have others that are useful at your institution.

- *Necessary expense.* This expense carries a contractual or legal obligation, or is *necessary* for the baseline existence of the organization. Examples here might be a building lease, an insurance policy on the collection, utilities, and so forth. This supports a "shell" of an organization, and isn't ideal in the long run, but is sustainable for approximately six months to one year. The definition of necessary expenses will vary tremendously by organization. Government and university museums may have the luxury of not paying directly for rent or maintenance, for example. Private museums will have a much larger percentage of expenses in this category.
- *Important expense.* These expenses make the institution what it is and are typically related to the mission. An example is a basic public programming budget. If you didn't have these expenses, you would question why the organization actually existed. Living on a budget that includes only these expenses would be sustainable for several years, but would create a dulled-down organization. You might find ways to work within this budget but would have to implement significant creativity to provide the public mission you once did.
- *Discretionary expense.* These are expenses that are really not necessary to fulfill the basic mission of the organization. They may, however, be necessary to fulfill the *vision* of the institution. These expenses may allow you to extend outreach, create new programs, or provide top-level collections care. If your budget was already very tight, you may not have any discretionary expenses at all. If your budget was flush, you might have a lot of expenses in this category.

Note how closely these budget categories align with mission and vision. Mission and vision are the tools that may help you assess which expenses are important or discretionary. They might even help you assess if expenses are necessary. As an extreme example, an institution might even reconsider whether a brick-and-mortar building is truly necessary to fulfill its mission. If your mission and vision aren't clear (or don't exist), and aren't distinct from each other, then you may discover that your budget priorities aren't very clear either. This exercise could be done by two institutions with a comparable budget, and the outcome would be very different.

As you evaluate your budget, you might find that an expense falls into several categories or needs to be "carved" up to be accurate. For example, having a certain number of public programs a year could be an important expense. Having a live musician or catered food at those programs might be a discretionary expense. I would recommend that you don't spend too much time trying to parse out the numbers or be precise. This exercise is about your priorities and is intended to spark discussion, so it's enough to have a rough idea of how you would categorize these costs.

The other caveat is that revenue may be dependent on expenses in some cases. For example, a public program may create revenue as well as incur costs. This exercise focuses on expenses because it's assessing how you use resources (not necessarily how you obtain them). Actual decisions about reducing a budget would need to factor in more complex considerations, such as if reducing an activity would also reduce income.

While staffing is usually a significant expense for an institution, staffing costs are not included in this example. There might be some exceptions, where staffing costs are dedicated to a particular program, for example. Staffing decisions carry a tremendous ethical responsibility, since they have such an impact on the livelihood of individuals. Some institutions also have restrictions about how funds can be used, which may mean they can't simply transfer funds to and from the staffing budget for other purposes. So, while staffing priorities are an important consideration, I recommend making it a separate discussion to give it the thought it deserves.

You can do the baseline budget exercise on your own, but the real benefit comes when you complete it as a team. On an individual basis, give the expenses some thought, categorize them, maybe jot down some justifications. Then ask a close colleague or a small team to do the same. Do your categories agree? Do they differ? Great, now you have the basis for an enlightening budget discussion! Talk it out. Why do you view expenses differently? Do your answers relate back to an institutional plan? Maybe there are some turf wars going on (my program is more important than yours)! What might the organization look like on a budget of this size? Do you have creative ideas for how you could overcome cuts of this size? Does your strategic plan or the mission of the organization clarify where resources should be prioritized? Could your director or board provide direction in this situation? A lack of clarity in this area can reveal a lack of alignment, strong opinions, and even infighting! Congratulations, you're budgeting with passion! While this can be difficult to talk through, it's better to have these conversations before these decisions actually have to be made.

This exercise can accomplish several things. First, it facilitates advance planning so you can better prepare for future downturns. If you've been in the museum field for a while, you've probably discovered that budgets are cyclical. Giving patterns change, state or city budgets get cut, and the stock market falls. These things will all affect your budget. So, it's almost inevitable that your institution will have to make reductions at some point in the future. It can be very taxing to make reductions without advance planning. While you can't possibly anticipate everything that will happen, an exercise like this one helps you prepare.

Another benefit is that you begin to compare your expenses to your institutional plan and priorities. This is where things can become interesting. Are you using your resources in the way you should? Is discretionary spending serving the highest use to further your vision? Or are you spending discretionary dollars on old programs or outdated practices that need renewal? On the other hand, are your "necessary" expenses, such as a lease, too high, which leaves little room for fulfilling your mission?

This exercise will also give you some interesting insight into how your colleagues, and museum leadership, view your resources. Does it reveal any mismatches between the organization's values and individual priorities? Are some people looking to the future, while others are valuing the past? Has a lack of resources created a competitive or distrusting environment? Or is your organization fortunate enough to have a surplus, which may have caused apathy about resource management?

As with all discussions, it's important that all ideas and concerns are treated with respect and that you try to understand and validate what someone is expressing (even if you don't agree with their idea). Particularly for staff members who may not have ever participated in a budget discussion, a commitment to an open environment and mutual learning is essential. You can never forget that numbers represent people. To some staff members, even hypothetical discussions about budget cuts can be difficult. Money represents value in a sense and categorizing a program as discretionary may suggest that the program is not important. So, keep this in mind and treat reactions thoughtfully. As is often the case with money, they will sometimes reveal personal or professional concerns that have nothing to do with the budget at hand. This experience will vary at your organization, but I can't recall a budget discussion where something interesting didn't "pop out" in the wash. Be ready for it and treat it respectfully. You might learn something about your own underlying values as well.

Adapting Your Horizon

The majority of institutions will budget on an annual basis, with quarterly reviews. This is a good format to use in most situations. There are times, however, when you'll find it beneficial to adjust your budgeting horizon to zoom in or out. In volatile or difficult times, I find it very helpful to reduce budgeting to a quarterly perspective. You should still try to get a fiscal year budget on paper but your focus will be on budgeting for the coming quarter. You might even reduce it to a monthly perspective if necessary. This is an approach for when you face a lot of uncertainty for reasons outside of your control. You'll of course want to create a longer plan, as well, but even in challenging situations you can usually predict a quarter's worth of expenses and revenue.

In the other direction, you may find that one fiscal year is just not enough to see around the corner. Particularly when embarking on a new strategic plan or when planning a long initiative, you may be better served to create a three- or five-year budget. This plan will be fuzzy around the edges for the distant years but will create a written commitment and projection for the future. Longer-term budgets can be a great way to commit to progress on initiatives that can't be implemented immediately. They also work well for certain sections and departments, such as exhibitions, who may plan their schedule several years in advance. In this situation, the upcoming year would have more detail and accurate projections. Then the rest would take shape as more is known and the timeline gets closer.

Creating Scenarios

In uncertain financial times, it's helpful to create detailed projections about how revenue and expenses might change over the coming quarter or fiscal year. It can be very challenging to predict these trends during large economic shifts. One method of creating projections is to plan three scenarios—optimistic, middle case, and pessimistic. These will help you understand how bad it might be, as well as how it might turn out if you're fortunate. Creating scenarios is a tried-and-true method for managing uncertainty, but I would recommend adding more detail for meaningful projections.

For example, in the category of revenue, you could easily project that the pessimistic scenario is a 20 percent drop in revenue for the next fiscal year. That might be a reasonable starting point and helpful as a quick calculation. Unless it's based on something tangible, however, it's really just a guess and may not be very accurate. Imagine how difficult it will be if the drop is really 50 percent, for example. In order to provide more depth to your projections, I instead recommend looking carefully at each revenue category and analyzing the likely level of volatility and timing of impact. If you're crunched for time, then focus on the largest categories that your museum relies on the most.

For example, our museum relies on endowment income for a substantial portion of its operating budget. Because endowments are invested, they follow the trends of the stock market and may have volatile swings. If that's all you knew about our endowments, you might conclude that this is an area where we would see significant downturns during difficult economic times. Yet, this actually isn't a problem because our endowments are "smoothed" over a sixteen-quarter period. So even negative returns for an entire year won't have an immediate impact on our endowment income. This is reassuring and means that endowment income will stay steady, or that decreases will be gradual. So, the worst case here is only a modest drop, at least for a one-year horizon. If problems continue, then we'll have time to adjust to the fact that our endowment income will eventually drop.

Earned revenue, on the other hand, changes very rapidly and in direct proportion to how well our store is doing. Yet, in our museum, earned revenue is a very small percentage of our operating revenue and designated for specific activities. And it can't really post a loss (we may not earn that much money, but it's also hard to actually lose it because we can also limit expenses). So, I can zero this category out and feel reasonably confident that this is the worst-case scenario for this revenue type.

Some categories are harder, however. If you rely on government funding, then you may anticipate a cut but have difficulty determining the timing and severity. For this, you might review your institutional history to see if you can find documentation on a previous cut. Or, assuming you're not in a severe situation, you might use a reasonable number such as 10 percent. Fortunately, cuts to government funding tend to roll slowly downhill, giving you adequate time to prepare.

You'll notice that these conclusions will be based on having a solid understanding of how your revenue works and the safeguards (or lack of them) that the revenue categories have in place. Even so, none of your projections will be perfect. But by assessing each category separately, you'll create a more nuanced and accurate overall projection. And you'll ferret out any potential surprises. You can also better understand which ones you should be actively monitoring, and which ones you only need to check on occasionally.

If you pair this exercise with the baseline budget exercise, you'll have a fairly good projection of revenue as well as an estimate of what it actually takes to run the institution. This will allow you to face a difficult financial situation with a sense of confidence. Despite your best efforts, you can't always control or predict what will happen. Taking a hard look at what it costs to run your institution and how your revenue is likely to be affected, however, can better prepare you for difficult times.

Conclusion

Budgets are dynamic and powerful engines behind the strategic plan of an institution. They're also concrete tools that can begin to address the inequities of our field. By engaging with budgeting, you can become a greater advocate for your own career and institution. You can better understand how resources are distributed, how budgets relate to your own priorities, and how to help your institution survive or even thrive. You might even find budget management kind of fun. My hope is that by getting more comfortable with terminology and budget concepts, you've gained more confidence to become a part of the discussion in the field. We all benefit when more voices contribute to the museum field's most important planning tool: the budget.

Appendix

Thirty-Three Ways to Expand Your Financial Knowledge

1. Try to identify your personal associations and memories associated with money. Can you recall times when money served you or your community, or brought you joy?
2. When you think about budgeting, what are the three words that first come to mind? Do they provide any insight into how you manage money in your personal or professional life?
3. Identify one or two motivations for increasing your knowledge of budgeting.
4. Describe your museum's budgeting process in three words. For example, transparent or opaque, interesting or boring, accessible or confusing.
5. Describe your museum's culture or important values in three words.
6. Are the two sets of words similar? If not, identify some small, concrete steps you can take to bring your core values into the budgeting process.
7. Find an older strategic plan for your institution. Do the objectives look familiar? How many of the initiatives did the museum achieve or complete?
8. Look over a recent budget and see if you can find tangible evidence of your strategic initiatives.
9. Look at your most recent strategic plan and review the resource allocation. Was it realistic and enough support for what you had hoped to achieve?
10. Find a completed, small project budget at your institution. Review how expenses are categorized and if the project stayed on budget.
11. Review the organizational chart for your organization. Does it mirror the section or departmental budgets? For example, if you have a curatorial section, do you also have a curatorial budget?
12. Find out what financial system your organization uses for reporting purposes.
13. Review a recent annual report to understand how section or department budgets are structured at your institution.
14. Try to learn about purchasing policies at your institution. Is there a dollar amount threshold for when purchases require approval?

15. Talk to someone who manages a section or department budget at your institution, and learn how they approach planning and budget review.
16. Learn what type of year your museum uses for budgeting (fiscal or calendar) and the dates of the budget cycle.
17. Even if you don't manage a budget at your institution, ask to observe an upcoming budget meeting.
18. See if you can find a copy of an internal quarterly budget report for your institution to see how the information is presented.
19. Choose at least one financial term to learn about in more depth. Search for the term online, read related articles, and use it in a few sentences (even if you're talking to yourself).
20. Teach someone else about one of the concepts that's new to you.
21. Find an annual report for your museum (or another) and try to find these terms in the text.
22. Find a financial blog or website that seems accessible and subscribe to it or read the top five articles.
23. Look up the living wage in your city (if there is one), as well as the median salary for your position in the museum field. You can find this through salary surveys published by the large professional organizations in the field.
24. Think about something you'd like to negotiate for and take time to build a compelling argument about how it would benefit the *other* party.
25. Locate a recent financial or annual report for your museum. Try to determine the largest categories of funding and revenue.
26. If you can compare year to year on a financial report, do the amounts change substantially in any of the categories?
27. Using the financial report, try to determine if your museum has mostly stable or mostly variable funding. If you were in charge of developing your museum's funding model, where might you put the emphasis?
28. Go online and find an annual report for a museum similar to your own. Does it appear that the museum has enough funding to cover expenses? Is there a surplus or deficit represented?
29. What are some of the budget challenges the institution is facing? You might find supporting information in the report narrative.
30. What is the budgeting process like? Can you tell who's involved and how decisions are made? Who is the report addressed to?
31. Review any earned revenue initiatives at your museum. Can you see the connection to the museum's mission?
32. Choose one fund to focus on and learn more about. If you don't have access to the financial information or original terms and conditions, you might still be able to learn about the fund's purpose and what type of activities it supports.
33. Begin to develop a brief narrative and working budget for a project you'd like to pursue.

Index

About the Author

Kristine Zickuhr is the chief operating officer at the Chazen Museum of Art, University of Wisconsin–Madison, and has been in the museum and historic preservation field since 1998. She holds an MA in art history and an MBA from the University of Wisconsin–Madison. During her career, Kristine has managed multi-million-dollar budgets, collaborated on a business plan for a new history center, and prepared numerous capital and biennial budget requests. She strives to make budgeting more accessible and relevant by welcoming all staff members into financial discussions.

CPSIA information can be obtained
at www.ICGtesting.com
Printed in the USA
BVHW012003230322
632130BV00006B/4